Blue Lights in the Night

Real Life Stories of a Maine State Trooper

Mark E. Nickerson

North Country Press

Blue Lights in the Night

Library of Congress Control Number: 2013936394

ISBN 978-0-945980-70-4

Edited by Beth Staples

North Country Press
Unity, Maine

I dedicate this book to my Dad, Millard E. "Nick" Nickerson, Jr. His life was one that I aspired to have. He grew up in Sanford, Maine, joined the U.S. Navy and fought in the Pacific as a naval flyer in World War ll. After coming home from the war he eventually joined the Maine State Police. He was one of the original State Police Detectives formed in 1955. He retired in 1973 as Captain, being the director of the Bureau of Criminal Investigations.

Mark's father presenting him with his badge.

To me, my Dad was larger than life in a quiet unassuming way. He played a major role in a very important job. I always wanted to be just like him. I can only imagine his reaction to my writing of this book.

I am also dedicating this to Maxim "Mickey" Squiers and his wife, Simone, who took me in, fed me, and treated me like family when I first went to Greenville all alone at the ripe old age of 22 as a young rookie trooper. Our friendship today is as strong as it was 35 years ago. Thank you!

Acknowledgments

I would like to thank all my family, especially my son Max, including my two ex-wives, for putting up with me in this crazy job. Even though the road wasn't always rosy, I was able to pursue my career with vigor, putting in a lot more hours than ever required by the department. There were lots of sacrifices by the family due to my working nights, weekends and holidays when most other people are off and enjoying time with their families. I know they had to go without many times as I missed special occasions.

To the other troopers that I worked with....each and every one of them have a book in them from the experiences they too have endured. They deserve my appreciation and thanks for all the camaraderie while dealing with some of the most trying times. But there were also some of the most unforgettable times provided by these same troopers. One thing we all had in common was the dedication to serve the public and make things right in the world as best we could.

And finally to Beth Staples, for her suggestion and finally encouragement to write the columns in her paper. Without her support, this writing thing never would have happened. Today, I wouldn't trade it for anything. It has brought so much enjoyment to me listening to the many people that I have entertained over the years.

Foreword

It came as no surprise to me when I learned that Mark Nickerson was writing a book about his experiences as a Maine State Trooper. I knew that Mark had kept all of his old diaries, copies of traffic accident reports, criminal investigations, hundreds of photographs and lots and lots of field notes.

Mark was raised in a State Police family. His dad, Millard Nickerson, joined the force in the 1950s and became one of New England's premier homicide investigators. When he retired as a Captain he was the commander of the Bureau of Criminal Investigation, or BCI, which today is referred to as the State Police Major Crimes Unit.

Mark entered his teen years watching his Dad and his squad of detectives travel from Kittery to Fort Kent solving some of Maine's most gruesome crimes. From these experiences Mark learned about hard work, sacrifice, disappointment and the simple satisfactions that come from helping others in their greatest time of need. Indeed public service was in Mark's blood so it was inevitable that soon after turning 21 years of age he applied to become a Trooper.

Mark graduated from the 34th Maine State Police Academy in the fall of 1977. First assigned to Troop C (Skowhegan) and later Troop D (Thomaston), Mark quickly developed a knack for finding and arresting drunk drivers. It was not at all uncommon for him to arrest three in one night and he took a great deal of pride in knowing that the roads were safer because of his efforts.

Mark was also a very curious person. He displayed a great sense of humor, genuinely liked people, loved talking to just about anyone and had a way of making others feel at ease. For Mark these character traits served him very well. He developed an effective network of criminal informants and as a result he solved crimes big and small. People told him things because they trusted him. People confessed to him because they liked him. It was that simple.

While I had met Mark on a number of occasions in the 1970s and early 1980s, it was not until April of 1985 that we had the opportunity to actually work together. I was promoted to Sergeant and assigned to Troop D. For the next two years Mark Nickerson was one of the eight Troopers in my section and as a result I got to know him well.

I quickly learned that Mark was a very hard worker and had an excellent grasp of what was taking place in his patrol area. I also found out that he was very set in his ways and could be as stubborn as anyone I had ever met. In the summer of 1985 the federal Fair Labor Standards Act (FLSA) was enacted and most members of the State Police transitioned from being on call 24 hours a day for six consecutive days to working 12 hours a day for those six days. While this schedule change was widely embraced by the rank and file, Mark personally hated it. He insisted that it would render him less effective as he would lose touch with the people in his patrol area. But he also hated it because he was assigned a specific shift and every second week he actually had to wake up early to get to work on time. That was not Mark's style. He was used to doing things his way and was not at all open to change. As his new Sergeant I was tasked with finding a way to have Mark conform. His peers in our section were watching with interest and my boss, the Troop Commander, was insisting on compliance. How did we do it? Compromise. Mark promised that he would "sign on" by radio at the beginning of his shift so that dispatchers and others would hear him but would then go back inside his home to prepare himself for the day. He held up his end of the agreement but continued to make it clear to me and anyone else that would listen that he didn't like it. He also continued to often work outside of his regular shifts so that he could, as he was fond of saying, "take care of things in his patrol area."

Mark and I also compromised on other aspects of State Police protocol. He had a disdain for wearing his State Police *Stetson* as required by policy. We found middle ground by him promising to wear it when either the Troop Commander or I was present. When we were not with him I was under no illusion that he was wearing that hat. Yes, Mark did things his way but continued to produce impressive results.

Mark was motivated not by opportunities for career advancement but by the need to make a difference in his patrol area. He had little interest in becoming a supervisor but took significant pride in reducing the percentages of OUI-related crashes or by increasing the clearance rates of crimes against people and crimes against property. He tracked his own local trends and kept his own statistics. He developed his own internal actions plans; independent of Troop priorities or statewide strategies. He was very "old school" in that sense and truly saw himself as the Chief of Police of the dozen or so small towns in his assigned area. As his Sergeant I couldn't argue with the outcomes that he produced.

Mark was one of the best drivers that I knew. He had a knack for teaching others too so it was a natural evolution for him to become a driving instructor at the police academy. He did it for a long time and did it well. He liked to drive fast too; even when it wasn't always necessary. As I recall he didn't always do so well with that and perhaps we will hear more about it in this book.

While I was his Sergeant I asked Mark to serve as a Field Training Officer (FTO) for recruits just graduating from the academy. He didn't like some aspects of the assignment, like rising early for a day shift, but he did a great job. Mark took the responsibilities seriously and knew that his efforts in those formative months for a recruit could literally make or break a rookie's career. He called it like he saw it and did not hesitate to speak up when he thought someone should not advance from their probationary status. I respected Mark for his candidness and for his honesty and put significant weight on his advice and counsel.

While I was Mark's field supervisor for only two years, I never forgot his independent nature. As a supervisor I knew that my job was to challenge each member of the section to reach their full potential. To truly achieve that

Mark taught me that it is important to be flexible. Later in my career, when deciding the appropriate level of discipline for policy violations, I always tried to look at the entire person and to put the non-compliance matter in its proper context. During those deliberations I inevitably thought of Mark and of our many debates about the need for formal rules and procedures.

In Maine, few troopers spend their entire career doing rural patrol work. Fewer still do it while remaining productive to the very end. Mark Nickerson is one of those few. He will tell you that he loved his job, his way of life, as much the day he left it as the day he started. What he grew weary of was all the "other" aspects of rural policing in the 21st century.

Maine's citizens are the beneficiaries of Mark's service. He had a very productive, interesting and rewarding career and many of those experiences are contained in his book. I look forward to reading it and sincerely hope that you do as well.

Colonel Malcolm Dow
Chief, Maine State Police, Retired

Mac Dow enlisted in the Maine State Police in 1976 and was first assigned to Troop F (Houlton) patrolling the Patten area. He rose through the ranks to serve as Deputy Chief (Lt. Colonel) from 1993 to 1997 and Chief (Colonel) from 1997 to his retirement in 1999. Following his retirement, Colonel Dow entered the private sector, where he continues to work as Director of Corporate Security for Irving Oil (New England & Atlantic Canada). He and his wife Susan reside in Hollis Center, Maine.

Table of Contents

Introduction

This whole writing thing happened quite by accident. I got a call one day from Beth Staples, who was the editor of "The Citizen," a local paper out of Belfast that served mostly Waldo County. She commented that my dear friend, John Ford, seemed to relish his occasional insults thrown at me when he wrote his columns "Memories from a Game Warden's Diary." Beth was wondering if I might have a story or two about John that I would be willing to share with the readers of "The Citizen." I told Beth that a few came to mind rather quickly but I was not too sure if I should share them just yet, still being an active duty Maine State Trooper. Beth assured me that she would edit the story and make sure I didn't get into too much trouble.

So my first story was written and published in the paper. The response was positive and quite flattering from the public. It was also immediate from my then-Colonel, Craig Poulin, who emailed and told me "Please tell me you don't have any more of these stories." I was within weeks of retiring so I knew I could probably get away with one more before pulling the plug. So the second one was written, although much tamer. I retired from the State Police on July 30, 2005 and my writing career, with Beth's encouragement and John's dismay, was on its way.

Writing these stories has been like living my career all over again. I always tried to see the humor in life's predicaments and keep a positive outlook. My career, to me, was fun. There were many harrowing incidents and times I wondered if I was going to come out the other side alive. From my first OUI arrest to my very last one, 1,363 drunk drivers later, it was a wild ride and one I wish I could do all over.

I was raised in a Maine State Police family, my father being a Maine State Trooper enlisting in 1953, becoming one of the first State Police detectives in 1955 and retiring in 1973 as Captain and director of the Bureau of Criminal Investigation. My father was larger than life to me and I relished every moment I got to spend around him and his career. As a boy I got to meet many of the legends of the State Police. Men like Eddie Marks, Merle Cole, Robert Marx, Lloyd Hoxie and many, many more. I wanted to be like them and live the life they did.

Against my Dad's wishes, but wanting to follow in my Dad's shoes, I pursued that career with the Maine State Police, becoming a trooper in 1977, and enjoyed just about every minute of it. One of my proudest moments being a trooper was my Dad pinning my badge on me at the Academy, and Dad telling me on his deathbed that pinning that badge on me was one of the greatest moments of his life. I miss him sorely but he taught me well. To always treat people with respect and to treat anyone the same way you would want to be treated. To be firm, but fair. Just because someone is doing something wrong doesn't always make them a bad person.

My Mom and Dad met during World War II, when my mom attended Nasson College in Springvale, Maine. She was raised in Hulls Cove and being in Springvale was a long way from home. She boarded with the Nickersons in

Sanford to save money and had little interest in my Dad until he returned home from Navy basic training. After the war ended, they were married, eventually making their way to Vassalboro, Maine, my Dad's first assignment with the Maine State Police.

As a young boy, I remember my mom had to take classes every Saturday to keep her teaching certificate current. So on Saturday mornings, being towed by Dad, my brother and I got to hang out at the State Police garage in Augusta. I got to meet the true legends of the department, wash cruisers, and play in an actual civil defense tank that was kept at the garage. The burning desire for me to become a state trooper started at a very early age.

I entered college in the pre-med field. I hated it. I had no interest in being a dentist. It was my Dad's wish. After failing miserably, I finally told my parents the only thing I wanted to be was a trooper like Dad. I changed my major and got a degree in criminal justice and public administration. Upon graduation from the University of Maine, my application process to the state police was already under way. But I had a problem. My eyesight was not 20/20 and I was worried that I would fail any eye test given to me. I wore contact lenses and whenever I was tested for my vision, I slightly fibbed about wearing contacts. But I passed all the tests. Lucky for me the contact lenses were never discovered.

My first assignment after getting out of the Academy in November 1977 was Greenville in Troop C. Truly frontier country if ever there is any left in the state. It was a magnificent place to live and work, although there were many hardships to this location as well. Winters hung on an extra month every year and it was a long way to go to see a movie. But I loved it there. The pay was a whopping $210 a week after getting out of the Academy. You were on duty 24 hours a day, six days a week, with a minimum of 10 hours per day on the road and you were subject to call out for all the other hours. Sometimes I would be gone from the house for days before getting back. The rest of the time was used for report writing, cleaning the cruiser, your gear and sleep. There were no portable radios, pagers, cell phones or computers. You had to be either at a phone or on the radio. Period. If they couldn't find you, all hell would break loose.

I got to meet and work with a man by the name of Maxim "Mickey" Squiers. Mickey started his career in law enforcement at the ripe old age of 50 for the Greenville Police Department. We spent many, many hours in my cruiser. He could start a story, and I could take a 15 minute catnap, wake up and he would still be telling the same story. I really liked it when I would stop one of his friends for OUI, look back at the cruiser and see Mickey hoofing it in the opposite direction so the drunk driver wouldn't see him. We had many laughs together.

In 1982 I transferred to Unity in Waldo County, where I finished out my career with the Maine State Police. My partner in crime then became Warden John Ford. How we ever made it to the end of our careers unscathed is beyond me. And there were times when I wondered if we were ever going to make it out of some incidents alive.

At the end of my career, the words of Col. Allen Weeks rang true. It is definitely a ringside seat to the greatest show on earth! So sit back and enjoy these true stories of my career. You can't make this stuff up. Most names have been changed to protect the privacy of the victims.

Clearing the Air

Due to encouragement from my friend Beth Staples, editor of the local Waldo County paper, and to the dismay of my other friend, Warden John "John Boy" Ford, my writing career commenced with this story. Please sit back and enjoy this ride through some highlights of my career.

In the mid-1980s, I received a call one night from Maine State Police dispatch in Augusta about a suspected OUI driver who seemed lost and kept pulling into driveways on Route 220 in Liberty. I was given a description of the vehicle, along with a partial license plate number.

John was along for the ride that particular evening and we were 20-25 miles away when we headed toward Route 220 in Liberty to try to find this possible OUI driver. Just after crossing Route 3 in Liberty and heading south, the first vehicle I met fit the description of the suspect. I turned on the vehicle and made the traffic stop just south of the Route 3 intersection. It should be noted I was suffering very badly with a cold on that particular evening--and this matters as the story goes along.

I approached the operator, who was alone in the vehicle. It became very obvious the middle-aged man was extremely intoxicated. I asked for a license and registration. The operator was able to produce a license, albeit with great difficulty.

I asked the operator, whose name was Earle, to step out of his vehicle. I could tell he was quite the character. He was from the coastal town of Waldoboro, and I was very familiar with his last name; troopers in that area dealt a lot with his family. He acted like a fisherman just off a boat after being at sea way too long. He was drunk, had a twinkle in his eye and was looking for some fun trouble. As he got out of his vehicle, Earle said his name wasn't Earle, it was Oil and if I didn't call him Oil, he was not going to answer me. So I told Oil to grease himself right into the right front seat of my cruiser so I could speak with him further. Oil did as he was asked and we both got into the cruiser. Johnny was sitting in the rear seat behind Oil.

Usually when processing an OUI, I filled out a form and asked routine questions. We both could tell it was not the first time Oil had enjoyed an alcoholic drink. Because of my cold I could not smell the alcohol on his breath, but I could easily tell he was pickled. There were a lot of other clues present than just the odor of alcohol.

I had a jar of Vicks between the seats to help me breathe. As I filled out the OUI report, Oil asked if he could borrow the Vicks. I had no idea why he would want to but I told him to go ahead. What could be the harm of that, right?

Out of the corner of my eye, I saw Oil pick up and open the jar. I continued to write, then suddenly a hand emerged from the passenger side seat and smeared a big blob of Vicks on my right side pant leg.

As John Boy told me later, I looked down at my leg, shot Oil a "What the heck did you do that for?" look, folded up my notebook, placed it on the dash board and, in one smooth move, landed on Oil in the passenger seat.

When I landed on him, the back of the bucket seat broke and the seatback, along with Oil's head, landed in John Boy's lap. As I was subduing the attacker, John Boy decided to take off Oil's glasses.

Oil briefly flailed about and realized he had made a mistake. He was ready to give up. I got off ol' Oil and he apologized as I handcuffed him and gave him a free ride to the Waldo County lockup in Belfast.

As we were traveling to Belfast, Oil said he couldn't see very well and asked for his glasses. John Boy produced them from the back seat and I put them on Oil's head.

We continued toward Belfast and Oil started to complain he was having a very difficult time seeing and that he was getting dizzy. This was disconcerting and I wondered if I had actually hurt ol' Oil. I looked at John Boy and quietly told him, "Jeez, I know I didn't hurt him any, just held him long enough to take the fight out of him."

John chuckled in the back seat, like only John can. He didn't really say much but I suspected something might be up. He was, and is, a pro at playing practical jokes.

We arrived at the county jail and as I escorted Oil inside, he stumbled into doorframes and walls. I again told John there was no way I had hurt Oil and he had to be faking it.

Oil continued to complain about his blurry vision and John finally exploded with laughter—giggles so loud he awakened the other prisoners.

I asked John what was so funny and he announced that after he took off Oil's glasses in the cruiser he smeared

Vicks all over them. John and I left the facility without telling Oil just why his vision was impaired.

I turned the report in as a routine OUI; attorney Lee Woodward, Jr. thought he had a good case. He pleaded him out. When the court news hit the papers, it showed that Oil paid the normal fines, plus restitution for a new pair of pants for Trooper Nickerson. I got a number of inquiries from people as to the unique restitution, but never told anyone. Until now, that is.

Just a quiet evening in the life of a trooper!

My Very First Drunk Driver

The Moosehead Lake region in Troop C was my first assignment after I graduated from the Maine State Police Academy in November 1977.

I remember getting my assignment from the colonel, then running to the map with most of the other recruits to see where we were headed. I had never heard of Greenville and was surprised to see where I was going.

However, after my first visit to the area, I was pleasantly surprised to see how beautiful it was. I quickly arranged to rent the upstairs of the Maine Warden chief pilot's house in Greenville Junction.

After reporting for duty, I was assigned to ride along with Trooper Paul Davis of Sangerville. He was to be my field training officer. Even though I had just spent 16 weeks in the academy, training was not over. For about 30 days we were on probation as we rode along with senior troopers and supervisors.

Trooper Davis was interesting to meet, to say the least. He had a very dry sense of humor and a natural ability to talk with people. And he was probably the worst driver with whom I ever rode. I learned a lot from him, and from the very beginning I was able to convince him that I should drive the cruiser. I somehow did this without offending him. However, he did have a favorite saying: "Nickerson, I'd rather be shot than scared to death!"

One of the first nights we rode together, I arrested my very first drunk driver. It was truly an eye-opener for a rookie like me. My parents reared me to respect police and obey the laws. I thought everyone was like this—boy was I in for a surprise.

On this particular night, it was very cold, and being in the mountains, there was already plenty of snow on the ground. Trooper Davis and I were in my cruiser, and I was driving.

As we headed south out of Greenville on Route 15, I came up behind a tan-colored Jeep that was all over the road, first going fast, then slow. I told my field training officer that I thought we should stop the vehicle for suspicion of OUI.

Paul told me to go ahead and make the stop. I put the cruiser's blue lights on, but the Jeep did not stop. It didn't speed up, either; the driver continued, seemingly unaware I was behind him. So I slid up beside the Jeep and identified the driver.

As I was beside him, the driver suddenly attempted to turn into a driveway on the right, which we later learned was his driveway. He missed the driveway and landed on top of a snow bank.

Both Paul and I were at his door before he could get out, so we helped him out of his vehicle. It was clear right away the driver was inebriated. His name was Greg, and he was not happy that he had been stopped.

Even though this was my first stop for OUI, it was an easy one to determine, as Greg was so drunk. We placed Greg in the back seat of the cruiser, while Paul and I got into the front. While Paul talked with Greg, I observed Greg's hand going for the door handle. I warned Paul that it looked like our catch of the night might be thinking about making a break for it.

No sooner had I said that when Greg jumped out of the back seat and made a mad dash for his house. I leaped out of the driver's side, and as soon as I rounded the back of the cruiser, I saw Paul on top of Greg in the snow bank.

To make matters worse, Greg had pushed his hands into the snow to make it more difficult for Paul to reach them. (Did I mention it was very cold that night?)

Paul yelled at me to get out my handcuffs. I took the cuffs out of the pouch and, to my horror, realized they were double locked — they couldn't be opened or closed without the key. And the key was in the cruiser.

Let me back up to the reason the cuffs were double locked. I graduated from the Academy the week before and my family had thrown me a party. At the party my middle brother, a terrible tease, kept cuffing his 5-year-old son. This, of course, made his son cry, so I took out the key and double locked them so my brother could no longer torment his son. Then I forgot all about double locking them when I went on duty.

Back to the story. Paul saw his rookie trooper running away from a fight and back to the cruiser, and he had no idea why. I was cussing up a storm at myself for being so stupid and unprepared.

In all the commotion, I could not get the handcuffs unlocked, so I ran back to help Paul, all the while still grappling with the handcuffs. Meanwhile, Greg screamed for his wife, Judy, to help him.

"Judy! Judy! Judy!" His voice echoed through the quiet North Country.

Judy came to the rescue. Wielding a broom, she ran out of the house and up the driveway. She started whacking Paul over the head with her broom.

Of course, I was still fumbling with the handcuffs. Finally, Paul pulled out his cuffs and we got Greg secured and back inside my cruiser. I was slightly overwhelmed by what happened. I thought all people respected law enforcement and would do as they were told to do. I couldn't imagine people would fight with the police.

I started the drive toward the jail in Dover-Foxcroft. The first three miles of the trip, Greg growled that he couldn't wait to see me hunting—that he was going to blister me right between the eyes. Thankfully, he passed out pretty quickly. I never really did take up hunting.

However, after he passed out, I got the butt-chewing of my career by my field training officer. "Young fella, you ain't in college anymore—this is the real world and you better get used to it if you plan on surviving the next 20 years."

After that incident, you can bet my handcuffs were never double locked again and that I checked my equipment before going to work. That OUI was the first of 1,363 drunks I removed from our highways in my career. And I have to admit, a lot of them provided quite a bit of entertainment.

Just a quiet eye-opening evening in the life of a trooper.

A Long, Sad Night

I'm going to tell you right up front there is no humor in this story. It was one of my toughest nights ever as a trooper, and it gave me extra purpose in my job and my life.

Friday, Dec. 21, 1979, started out like any other day. I was working a major criminal case in the Monson area of Piscataquis County and it was taking a lot of time, even though I had not yet scratched the surface of the case.

I spent most of the day between Greenville and Dover-Foxcroft, taking care of complaints, working on the major case, turning in paperwork and meeting with my sergeant. Around 12:20 a.m., I covered an accident in the Guilford area. As soon as I cleared that scene at 3 a.m., dispatch at Maine State Police HQ in Augusta sent me to Sandy Bay Township on Route 201 to assist Trooper David Viles with a head-on crash. Sandy Bay Township is north of Jackman, just south of the Canadian border.

I arrived at 4 a.m. and met with Trooper Viles. It was about 25 below with the wind chill factor. It had snowed some, and the road was covered with about 3-4 inches of snow.

The two vehicles involved were a northbound tractor-trailer unit with a single operator and a southbound pickup truck with four young males crammed inside the cab. The tractor-trailer was going down a hill with a slight right turn in it. The tractor-trailer had gone to the bottom of the hill and had come to rest in the right-side ditch. The driver was still in the rig.

The pickup truck had been struck so violently that it spun 180 degrees in its driving lane and came to a stop facing the opposite direction. After investigation, it was determined that due to bald tires on the rear of the trailer and slippery road conditions, the trailer had swung out into the opposite lane and struck the pickup head-on. The most aggravating circumstance was the driver of the tractor-trailer was under the influence of alcohol.

The tractor-trailer operator was not injured, but he had to be secured so he could not drink any more. A blood alcohol test had to be administered.

The four teenage boys did not fare as well. The pick-up was folded almost in half and all four boys were still inside. We could not get to them to assist them or get them out. We crawled through the wreckage to do what we could while waiting for better equipment to arrive. The driver had been killed, as had the boy sitting next to him. The third boy had life-threatening injuries. The fourth had injuries but they did not appear to be life-threatening. Our immediate problem was we could not get them out of the truck.

There was only one wrecker service in Jackman. We, of course, called him for assistance, thinking we could spread apart the pick-up and get to the boys. When the wrecker arrived, we learned the boy with life-threatening injuries was the son of the wrecker operator. We quickly escorted him away. We then waited for two wreckers to arrive from Skowhegan. We kept the boys warm and treated them the best possible way until we could get them out.

When the two wreckers arrived, they each got on one end of the pick-up, pulled it apart and we got the boys out of the truck. They were taken to the hospital for treatment and both survived.

After getting information on the two deceased boys and their families, Trooper Viles requested that I go to Jackman to make the death notifications. He was staying for further investigation and to clean up the scene.

I had a pretty good contact in Jackman and spoke with him so I could learn more about how to make these horrific notifications to the waiting families.

Many Jackman residents attended the local Catholic church and my contact advised me it would be wise to get the local priest to go with me to make the notifications. I did just that.

I went to the first residence to deliver the horrible news. It was as though they were expecting me. It was getting to be 6:30 a.m. Most of the family was at the kitchen table, which included mom, dad and others. I saw that familiar look on the dad's face when a police officer enters the home for no apparent reason except to deliver bad news.

All he said to me was, "He's dead, isn't he?"

"Yes sir, he is."

I told them where their boy was being taken and provided any information I could they might need. They thanked me for telling them, and I left their home. It was hard not to show any emotion to these people.

We went to the next family, which was the boy's mother. I had no idea what an impact this would have on me for the rest of my life.

11

I knocked on the front door and after waiting for a little while a middle-aged lady came to the front door and opened it. The terror I saw on her face was almost too much for me. To see a trooper and a priest at her door first thing in the morning was not going to be good news. The priest said hello to her. She replied to him without ever taking her eyes from me.

I told her I had sad news about her son. Without any type of warning she attacked, striking me in the chest several times with her fists and screaming, "Don't tell me he's dead!" She was crying hysterically, tears running down her face.

I wrapped my arms around her to keep her from hitting me. She hung on to me for all she was worth and sobbed. I lost it and cried with her. I have no idea how long we embraced and cried. But I let her do what she needed to do to console her.

Afterward, the priest told me he would stay with her and contact other family members. I left her home and never saw her again. But she made an impression on me that affected me for the rest of my career.

The facts of the crash were simple and deadly. Four boys from Jackman, some home from school for Christmas break, had decided to get together and have some fun in Canada. The boy who did not drink was the driver. After their fun, they all headed home to Jackman. They did nothing wrong.

The driver of the tractor-trailer was heading home to Canada. He had stopped at a bar in Jackman, drank too much booze, got into his rig and headed north on the slippery road with bald tires on the trailer. While coming down over a hill with a slight right turn, the trailer slid out into the opposite lane, striking the pick-up head-on and killing two of the boys.

Because the crash happened in a remote area, it was hours before it was discovered and reported. Even though the tractor-trailer operator's blood alcohol was 0.09 percent, we lost the manslaughter case in court.

After giving that death notification to that mother, I recommitted myself to go after drunk drivers as hard as I could for the rest of my career. No parent should ever have to be told their child has been killed by a drunk driver. I ended my career in the Maine State Police with probably more arrests for drunk driving than any other trooper, thanks, in part, to the mother in Jackman.

A Warm, Fuzzy Feeling

One evening I was called to a motor-vehicle crash on Mann Road in Palermo, a back road in Waldo County. I located the vehicle on its side in the ditch but there were no people around. After checking the vehicle for occupants, I started searching in the nearby woods to make sure no one had been ejected.

Finding no one, nor any evidence of anyone, I checked the vehicle further and found evidence of a possible injury. However, there were no signs of any illegal substances or alcohol being involved in the crash.

I called for a wrecker to remove the vehicle. While waiting, I surveyed the scene to learn why this vehicle left the roadway. I determined speed was definitely a factor. After checking the registered owner via the computer, I learned the driver might have been young and inexperienced. After the vehicle was removed and impounded by the wrecker company, I found the registered owner—a teenage boy—at his parents' home in East Vassalboro.

To me, this was a stroke of luck. It was a good chance to make an impression on the new driver and have the parents involved.

After I explained why I was there, the parents welcomed me into the home. They were aware of the accident and walked me into the kitchen to speak with their son. A beautiful, docile friendly golden retriever was in the kitchen, too.

The young boy got out his license and we went through how to fill out an accident report and the 48-hour form. While speaking with the boy, it was normal procedure to ask what happened and why he thought he crashed.

As he talked, I could tell he was very nervous, not so much from doing something wrong, but because of the accident and because he had never had a trooper in his home before. And all this had happened within a few weeks of getting his driver's license.

I understood his explanation and he admitted to going too fast for his driving skill level.

The real problem, though, was he had left the scene and not reported the accident to law enforcement by quickest means possible. And the more he spoke the more it became obvious that he clearly, intentionally violated that law. After the interview, the teenage boy left me no choice but to issue him a summons for failing to report the accident.

The parents supported their son, but realized he made a mistake. They understood the situation and knew I had no choice in my enforcement action. I got out the necessary paperwork to issue the boy a summons. Up to that point in time, that beautiful golden retriever had quietly sat on the floor, minding his own business. But when I stood at the kitchen counter writing out the summons, all of a sudden I felt something very warm and wet run down my leg.

I quickly looked at my leg and burst out laughing. The golden retriever was relieving himself on my right leg. Could this dog really know what had just transpired?

Everything was fine until I got out the summons book. It was as if the dog was saying "This is what you get for giving my master a ticket."

I looked at the parents who both had horrified looks on their faces. They didn't know what to do. They got towels, offered to wash my uniform, offered to pay for the dry cleaning and on and on. They said their dog had never done anything similar to this before.

I told them they would have a great story to tell their family and friends. I finished issuing the summons and kept a keen eye on the dog.

Just like Larry the Cable Guy might say, "I don't care who you are, this was funny!"

Just another day in the life of a trooper.

A Very Special Detail

Throughout my career with the Maine State Police, I could count on things never being the same from one day to the next.

Details had to be taken care of daily—buildings being moved that needed escorts and shifts that had to be filled, as did late-night OUI details and early-morning speed details. There were also off-duty court appearances and major crime scenes to be secured. The list went on and on.

These details were above and beyond the regular hours of duty. Some were exciting, while others were routine. Details were filled according to troop seniority and, being the old guy in the troop for so many years, I usually had the pick of all the details. Basically, I could make out my own schedule.

Our country's involvement in the war in Iraq had started to drain the Maine State Police resources, because so many troopers were also in the National Guard or directly involved with the military. Because so many of our officers were called to duty in Iraq, troopers in Maine felt connected to what was happening there. We had direct contact with some of the troopers serving, and got information in real time.

Then the worst happened. In December 2004, a suicide bomber struck a dining tent in Mosul, Iraq. There were many injuries and deaths, and two of the soldiers killed were from Maine—Sgt. Lynn Poulin Sr. of Freedom, and

Spc. Thomas J. Dostie of Somerville. They both served with the 133rd Engineer Battalion.

The president of our Trooper Association, Sgt. Mike Edes, immediately contacted all the troopers and requested we escort the bodies home from the airport.

Edes wanted Maine troopers to show to the citizens of the state and to the families of the fallen soldiers our support for soldiers serving in Iraq. He was looking for volunteers to do the escort. Needless to say, it did not take long to find enough troopers to get the job done.

I immediately put in to escort Spc. Dostie's body home from the Portland Jetport. I was chosen to do this detail along with a contingent of other officers.

I had to work on the day of the escort, but I was given permission from my supervisor to take the time for the detail. Spc. Dostie was from my area, and I would be able to lead the procession easier. I arrived at Maine State Police Headquarters in Augusta around 1515 hours to clean my cruiser then head south to meet with my supervisor, who also was involved in the escort. We met in South Portland, where we again cleaned the cruisers, as road conditions were poor.

Afterward, we headed over to the Jetport to wait for the plane. Todd Brackett, sheriff of Lincoln County and a couple of deputies were also present. Then the hearses arrived with the family. This was a very solemn moment, and I could tell it was going to be an emotional ride back with the family and our fallen soldier.

We arranged the vehicles, with my cruiser leading the procession. The sheriff was near the hearse, the family rode in the hearse, and the other Maine State Police cruisers followed behind. We jumped on the turnpike and headed north.

I did not want anyone to pass the procession. I thought it would show disrespect to Spc. Thomas Dostie. So, I led the procession into the passing lane and put the speed right at 65 mph. My supervisor felt the same and would not allow anyone to pass from the rear. This was just a small tribute we could pay to such a young hero. We also had other prearranged details along the way to show respect for the family and Spc. Dostie.

We drove north from Portland without incident, blue lights on. Everyone got out of our way, and no one came close to us from behind. The avenue we chose to go through in Augusta was the new exit north of Augusta and across the new bridge. We had four intersections to go through. At each intersection, four troopers had parked their cruisers to block all the traffic.

The troopers stood at attention and saluted as the hearse passed by. I dropped the speed down so the procession could travel slowly through each intersection so troopers could pay respects to this soldier.

Each of the troopers at the intersection then fell into line and followed the procession toward the funeral home in Windsor.

The procession had grown considerably. Looking back through my mirrors, all I could see was a line of blue lights. It put a lump in my throat and tears in my eyes and I thought, "What a wonderful way for us to honor such a man."

I did not have much time to think about the events; just before I arrived at the funeral home, I was called to reconstruct a fatal motor-vehicle crash in South Thomaston, where another young man had just lost his life. After delivering the procession to the funeral home, I left for the call. The events of the night certainly made me think about life.

A footnote about this story: While one of the troopers blocked an intersection in Augusta, an angry motorist called State Police Headquarters to complain about being held up for no apparent reason. The motorist demanded to speak with the trooper's supervisor. A short time later the same motorist sheepishly called back to say he no longer wanted to make a complaint and he apologized for calling in the first place. He realized why the intersection had been momentarily blocked.

My Barney Fife Moment

After having two days off in June 1979, I returned home and crawled into bed around 3 a.m. I looked forward to crashing and sleeping in.

Back then, we had 24-hour duty. We were required to put in 10 hours per day on the road—the 10 hours we put in were our choice, so long as State Police Headquarters could find us to call us out during the other 14 hours. I knew they could find me asleep in my bed.

At about 7 a.m. I got a call from SP Augusta Headquarters.

"Hi, Mark?"

"Yes?"

"We have a call from a storeowner in Kokadjo that a fugitive we've been looking for just left his store and drove north toward the Golden Road. He is driving a tan Monza, and he has a female passenger with him."

"Is this the escapee from the State Prison?"

"Yes. We believe it is."

"I'll be heading up!"

After I hung up, I started to go over in my head what I had learned before I left for two days off. Being the only trooper in the north country of Piscataquis County, a lot of people contacted me about suspicious activities or told me about things that didn't seem quite right.

For about a week, I had been told about a very large Native American and a blonde Caucasian woman. Both were reportedly very intoxicated, and it appeared the woman was being abused by the man. I had been told of a violent confrontation on the lawn of a hotel in Rockwood, but the couple took off before anyone called police. No one seemed to know who they were or where they were staying. I checked around with negative results. I did learn, however, there was an escapee from the Maine State Prison and this large Native American fit the description of the escapee.

I quickly donned my uniform and gear, jumped into the cruiser and headed out for the 20-mile ride to Kokadjo from Greenville. I arrived at the store to confirm what I had been told. The owner was someone I knew quite well and trusted.

He again told me who he thought the man was, and he described the female and the vehicle, along with the registration number. He also told me the suspect had headed north just before he called State Police HQ. The storeowner had no idea where the suspect was driving to but wished me luck.

There was one patron in the store that early morning. He and I did not get along. (That's another whole story.) The patron, "Bob," looked at me and snidely asked, "I hope you don't think you're going to get that big Indian all by yourself, do you?"

"No, the cavalry is on its way," I told him.

I left the store a little peeved that I had to put up with "Bob" so early in the morning and that he had made such a rude remark. But I blew it off as I had more important things to worry about at this moment. I jumped into my cruiser and headed into the North Country toward Ripogenus Dam.

After leaving the pavement beyond Kokadjo, numerous woods roads branch off the main dirt road. While driving, I kept thinking to myself, "Should I take a side road or keep going north?"

I decided to keep driving north as all the side roads dead-end anyway, and the wanted person would eventually have to come back out onto the main road.

I continued driving until I reached the Great Northern gate at Siras Hill. The gate is tended, and I knew I would be able to check with the keeper to see if the suspect had gone through.

Just as I came into sight of the gate, I saw the vehicle I was looking for. It was stopped, the gate was closed, the blonde was in the right front passenger seat, the Native American was driving, and the little old lady gate-tender was talking with the man through the passenger window. No one saw me drive up behind the suspect vehicle. So far, so good.

I kept my eyes glued on the man. I got out of my cruiser and started to approach him on the driver's side of the vehicle. I still had not been seen. While walking up to the suspect vehicle, I drew my service weapon and walked all the way to the driver's door without being noticed.

Once at the driver's door, with the man still looking out the passenger window, I stuck the gun right behind his ear, and stated in a voice that I had never heard before: "Do not move!"

I even scared myself!

25

What surprised me even more was that after telling the enormous man not to move, he turned around and looked right down the barrel of the gun. I kept telling him not to move and to put his hands on the steering wheel. Thankfully, he complied. Once he placed his hands on the steering wheel, I reached in and handcuffed him.

Again telling him not to move, I opened the door of the vehicle, reached in and grabbed the handcuffs. I told him to slowly turn and step out of the vehicle. All the while, I had my left hand on the handcuffs and my right hand held my gun on him.

What happened next was clearly the Barney Fife moment of my career.

As the man turned to get out of the vehicle and stand up, I thought there was no end to him. At the time, I was a pretty good-sized man, about 6 feet tall and pushing 200 pounds.

As the suspect stood up, he seemed to just keep growing. I kept looking up and up and up. He stood well over 6-6. He had long black hair to his shoulders, and it was obvious he was in very good shape. I think he was as scared as I was, as my gun started to shake when I saw how big he was. I think he was as worried as I was that my gun might go off at any moment. Even though I could read his facial expressions, he never uttered a peep.

To add to the confusion, the little old lady gatekeeper was about to pass out. She kept gasping and screeching. I tried my best to ignore her and concentrate on the escapee. I led him back to my cruiser. I walked backward, held onto the handcuffs, and pointed the gun straight up at his head.

I placed him in my cruiser, told him he was under arrest and that he was going to be taken to the county lockup in Dover-Foxcroft so state prison officials could get him. He never said a word.

I drove back to Kokadjo. I learned on the radio that Cpl. Paul Davis was driving north to meet with me, and he was bringing probation officer George McCormick with him. We met at the store in Kokadjo, and the prisoner was transferred from my cruiser into Cpl. Davis' cruiser, and he was whisked away. I certainly sighed a sigh of relief once he was gone from my cruiser.

I had just started to calm down from the sheer terror of how bad things could have gotten in a split second. So while at the store, I decided to go inside and thank the storeowner for his involvement.

We conversed for a little while, then I noticed "Bob" was still in the store. He looked at me with complete disgust and said , "I don't believe you just captured that guy all by yourself."

I looked at "Bob," picked at my teeth and said, "Yep, just lucky," then turned and left the store with a huge grin on my face.

I got in my cruiser and headed home to Greenville to go back to bed.

All I could think about driving south to Greenville was, "Isn't it amazing how life can be so peaceful, then filled with sheer terror, then back to peace and quiet again so quickly."

The Wave

One problem of being a trooper was there were just too few of us. Almost all the time, we were wanted or needed in a dozen places at once, and most of the time we had to get there quickly.

Late one evening, I was called to Augusta and had to make a quick trip from my patrol area into the city. I was driving into Augusta on Route 3 and came upon a much slower-moving vehicle.

I was probably following a little close, as I was waiting for a chance to pass. It seemed to take a while as there was no safe place to pass, so I waited until the right opportunity arose.

Finally, we reached the slow lane approaching the steep hill just east of Augusta and it was my chance to get by. I accelerated quickly and started to make a pass by the slow-traveling vehicle.

Just as I got beside the vehicle, a hand came up in the driver's side window and gave me "the finger!" I continued driving for a short distance then decided that maybe I should have a talk with this person.

I pulled into Lapointe Lumber's parking lot in Augusta and waited for the vehicle to go by, then I pulled out and activated the cruiser's blue lights. While approaching the vehicle, I saw it was being operated by a lone female about 20 years of age.

It was obvious she was sorry about what had happened. She did not make eye contact with me, and I could tell she regretted her action.

I asked for her license and registration and quickly recognized the name to be that of a very well-known Cony High School girls basketball alum. This woman was an aggressive firecracker when she played for the Rams. She had a reputation for being one of the best ball-handlers and defenders of her time. And it appeared that she was a firecracker off the court as well.

I was rather shocked at her behavior, but knowing my enforcement action was rather limited, I leaned into the window and simply stated, "The next time you wave to me, you need to use all your fingers, do you understand?"

"Yes, sir!" she replied.

"Now get out of here," I told her.

She was only too happy to disappear from my sight.

The rest of the story is the funny part.

Fast forward about 12 years. I met my brother, Mike, for lunch in Augusta one afternoon while on duty. I was in uniform and we met at the old Mike's Lunch on the east side. My brother had a friend who was going to meet us as well for lunch. My brother's friend, Jerry, arrived and told us that his girlfriend was going to be joining us soon. While eating lunch, Jerry's girlfriend arrived.

She sat down directly across from me and we were introduced. I remembered her name from the Cony girls basketball team from years before and yes, it was the same girl I stopped more than a dozen years earlier for waving to me without using all of her fingers.

I never let on about stopping her, and there was a lot of small talk and laughing. Finally Jerry's girlfriend said to me, "I see that you're a state trooper."

"Yes, I am."

"Well, I have this really funny story that happened to me years ago when a trooper stopped me."

"Oh, really?" I asked her, still not letting on I remembered it well.

She proceeded to tell me the whole story from her perspective. Of course she "waved" to me because she thought the driver had been following her too close, and when the vehicle passed her, she wanted to express her feelings.

But after the vehicle was by her and she saw it was a Maine State Police cruiser, she absolutely panicked. She said she was horrified when the blue lights came on and she was stopped. She said she thought for sure she was going to jail for flipping off the trooper.

"Do you know what the trooper said to me," she asked with a kind of smirk on her face.

I said, "I believe it was, 'The next time you wave to me, you need to use all your fingers.'"

After I said this, I sat there and watched her eyes bug out and her mouth hit the floor. She was speechless. I laughed and told her that I was the trooper who had pulled her over that night. My brother and his friend rolled on the floor laughing.

When she finally got her wits, she finished the story. She said she didn't breathe until the cruiser was out of sight, then burst out laughing over the whole thing and breathed a huge sigh of relief that she wasn't being taken to jail.

She said she was on her way to a party that evening and when she got there, she told her story to everyone. Apparently it was a party favorite for years to come!

Just another quiet evening on patrol.

Oh Dear, It Just Won't Die

I covered a lot of car-deer crashes through my career and did not like taking care of them.

It seemed as though in more than half the crashes, the deer was badly injured but not killed and had to be put down. I enjoy watching deer; I think they are beautiful animals, running and jumping gracefully through fields and into the woods. But I also understand how they can be a menace to drivers. What bothered me the most was having to put down injured deer. It seemed as though they looked me straight in the eye and wondered why I was doing this to them.

Sometimes I would go six or seven months without responding to any car-deer collisions. Then all of a sudden, eight to 10 deer in one night would get hit by vehicles. Throughout my career I, too, was the unfortunate driver who struck many a deer. But that's a whole bunch of other stories.

The car-deer story I want to tell you about was one that scared the crap out of me late one night.

It was 3 a.m. one late fall morning. I was sound asleep in my warm, cozy bed when the phone rang. Maine State Police Headquarters advised me of a car-deer crash on Rte. 139 in Unity, about a mile west of Unity Raceway. The deer was not dead, and there was extensive damage to the vehicle.

I climbed out of bed to respond to the scene. I threw on some pants, a shirt and my state police jacket and grabbed my gun belt.

The scene was not far from my home, so I thought I could skip over to it, take care of it, and slide right back home without missing a wink.

I arrived on scene within a few minutes and met with the operator of the vehicle. The scene consisted of a drivable vehicle with front-end damage parked in the breakdown lane. The deer, a 180-pound, eight-point buck was down on the edge of the road behind the vehicle. The driver, a very prim, proper, well dressed, middle-aged woman was upset over the condition of the deer.

I looked everything over and after checking the deer, I realized it had to be put down. This upset the lady even more as she thought that something better than killing him should be done. But I explained to her that one of his legs was broken and the humane thing to do would be to put him down. She finally agreed it was the right thing to do.

I never was much of a hunter but, due to my job, I had shot my share of deer. We were taught at the academy exactly where to aim to kill an animal with one shot. Most of the time this worked fine, although a few shots were sometimes necessary to kill a moose.

I warned the woman that if the shooting was going to bother her that she should stay in my cruiser so she would not have to witness it—which is what she did.

I went to the front of my cruiser and got in a good position to shoot the buck. I did what I had to do, and watched as the deer expired...or so I thought. I waited for awhile and all of a sudden the deer picked up his head. I again did what had to be done, shooting more than once that time. I finally was satisfied the deer had expired.

I got inside my cruiser and told the woman the deer was dead and we could do the paperwork. The driver, still upset over the deer being put down, produced her license, registration and insurance card, and I got busy jotting the information onto the accident report.

I kept my head down, reading the information as I filled out the form. I asked her several questions as required and everything was going routinely.

I was anxious to get the forms filled out and get her on her way, so I could get back to my warm, cozy bed. Just as I was finishing the report, the woman let out the worst blood-curdling screech I had ever heard. It startled me so badly that I jumped in my seat and banged my head on the ceiling of the cruiser.

"What's the matter," I screamed.

"Look! Look," she screamed and pointed out over the hood of my cruiser.

I regained my wits and looked out the windshield. There, standing in front of my cruiser with his head hanging over my hood and his eyes looking right at me was the deer that I had shot five times, the deer I twice thought I had killed. Well, apparently it scared me more than it scared her, and I screeched even louder than she was screeching.

After I stopped shrieking, I got out of the cruiser and finally dispatched the deer for good.

Needless to say, after getting home I never was able to get back asleep.

Just another quiet evening in Waldo County.

Giving a Hand

I always thought having a sense of humor should be a requirement in this job, because if you don't have one, you might be in for a long career.

I remember a story about a trooper in Montana who obviously had a good sense of humor and I thought I would share it. The story triggered me to remember a few comparable escapades of my own—just to show that we, too, have a sense of humor here in Maine.

This is the story I received about the Montana trooper: It was about 3 a.m. one very cold morning. Trooper Allan Nixon of the Montana Highway Patrol responded to a call about a car off the shoulder of the road outside of a small Montana town. The trooper located the car stuck in deep snow with the engine still running.

Pulling in behind the car with his emergency lights on, the trooper walked to the driver's door and found an older man passed out behind the wheel. A nearly empty vodka bottle was beside him on the seat.

The driver awakened when the trooper tapped on the window. Seeing the flashing lights in his rearview mirror, and the state trooper standing next to his car, the old man panicked. He jerked the gearshift into drive and hit the gas. The car's speedometer showed 20, 30, 40, then 50 mph, but the vehicle remained entrenched in place in the snow, wheels spinning.

Trooper Nixon began running in place next to the speeding, but stationary car. The driver was totally freaked, thinking the trooper was somehow keeping up with him. That went on for about 30 seconds, then the trooper yelled at the old man, "Pull over!"

The man obeyed, turned his wheel and stopped the engine. Needless to say, the man was arrested and is probably still shaking his head over the Montana state trooper who could run 50 mph.

The story brought to mind several drunk-driving arrests that I made and I thought I would share one with you.

Early one evening, I was called to a motor vehicle crash on the Level Hill Road in Palermo. I was aware of an annual spring beer bash being held farther up the road. I had full intentions of working it later that evening after other calls quieted down. However, it seemed as though things got going a little earlier than usual that year.

I was traveling to the accident scene and had just turned onto the Level Hill Road from Route 3. While going north, there is a long straightaway before a sharp right turn. The crash I was responding to was supposed to be at that sharp turn.

I was within a couple of hundred yards of the turn when suddenly another vehicle approached the sharp turn from the opposite direction.

I could see the vehicle involved in the initial crash just off the road in a field. The second vehicle was making its way around the turn and I could tell it was going way too fast to make it around the corner. And I was right. The second vehicle went into a slide, went off the road, sideswiped the first vehicle, sailed across a field and landed in a deep, tree-covered ravine.

I quickly pulled up alongside the field, snapped on my emergency lights and bailed out of my cruiser to check on the driver. I thought the driver would be injured. I remembered a fatal crash that had occurred on the very same corner just a few years earlier.

I ran through the field, and entered the wooded area, making my way down into the ravine. I finally came to the vehicle on its side. I climbed up on the vehicle and peered down through the broken-out window. The driver, who was alone, was regaining his senses about where he was and how he was going to get out of the vehicle.

From my vantage point, I could tell he wasn't hurt badly but it was obvious he was extremely drunk. I put my flashlight on him to check to see if he appeared injured. He was thrashing around, panicking about how to get out. I told him to calm down and that I would help him.

After he heard my voice, he blurted back to me, "Help me get out of here before the cops get here!"

"All right, well, give me your hand and let me help you up through the window," I told him. I thought that I would play along with this guy and not let on anything. Sooner or later he would see the uniform and figure it out.

He grabbed my arm and hoisted himself up through the window. It was pretty dark and I kept the flashlight on him and the area where we had to go, never shining it on me.

As we climbed off the car and got back on the ground, the driver kept talking. "Man, I can't afford to get busted for drunk driving again; and I am so drunk. I was up at the party and thought I would leave early before the cops started hanging around. I can't believe I crashed."

"Oh, really? How much did you drink up there, anyway," I asked him.

"I lost count after the first 10," he told me chuckling but still concerned about making a clean getaway from the cops.

I had him by the arm and was assisting him up the steep ravine when all of a sudden he saw my cruiser's blue lights flashing.

"Oh shit!" he whispered. Then he crouched down as if he was hiding from the blue lights.

I still had a hold of his arm and I thought it might be a good time to let him know who was helping him.

"What's wrong?" I asked him.

"I don't want the cops to find me."

"It's too late for that," I told him.

"What do you mean?"

I then turned the flashlight on myself and told him I was Trooper Nickerson with the Maine State Police and I would be assisting him the rest of the way to the cruiser.

It was just like popping a balloon with a pin. He exhaled and went limp. He also got arrested and went for a free ride to the county lockup in Belfast.

Just another quiet evening in Waldo County.

Looking For His Driveway

I watched a rerun of Jerry Seinfeld (one of my favorite TV shows) recently, during which Jerry's comedy routine touched on elderly drivers.

He said, "At what age do you have to be when you no longer look backwards when you back your vehicle up? You just back up and people either get out of your way or you hit something. After you hit something, then it's time to go forward."

I got quite a laugh from his routine—and then all kinds of flashbacks came to me of the elderly drivers I dealt with during my career.

As funny as most of them were, though, deep down it was sad. Most elderly drivers know driving is their last bit of independence, and they fight to the end to keep it.

My mom is in her early 80s and still drives. I tease her about taking her license, and boy does she give it right back to me. But it is a serious issue, as no one wants anyone to get hurt, including my mother.

It seems when some people get older, they tend not to look as far down the road while driving. We call this "driving at the end of your hood."

When doing building escorts, sometimes I would need both lanes, as the building would take up the whole road. I drove ahead of the building in the middle of the road and pushed oncoming traffic onto the shoulder.

This particular time, as usual, the cruiser's blue lights were on, as were the wig-wags—the headlights that alternately flash back and forth. They are usually brighter than blue lights during the day. Traffic slowed and moved over as I waved oncoming drivers onto the shoulder.

Sometimes, the elderly were the most difficult to deal with in that situation as they saw the cruiser but not what was behind it.

One day, an oncoming vehicle being driven by an elderly female approached my cruiser. I could see two hands near the top of the steering wheel and her eyes peeking out through the steering wheel. Her hands were higher than the top of her head. She would not pull over onto the shoulder and defiantly stayed in her driving lane. It was definitely a stand-off. She stayed put and I stayed in the middle of the road, waving her over.

Finally, out of frustration, I got out of my cruiser and approached her. She rolled down her window and had several not-very-nice words for me. The point of her rant was for me to get the hell out of her way! I told her to calm down and I would show her something. As she quieted down, I asked her if she could see beyond my cruiser.

"Of course I can, Sonny," she snapped.

"Well, what do you see?" I asked.

She looked down the road and strained her eyes, which then opened in complete surprise. It was like she had seen a ghost.

"It's a house!" she screeched.

"Yes, and that is why I have been waving you over so we can continue on."

She immediately apologized and moved her car onto the shoulder. After I got by her, I could only chuckle.

The funniest and saddest incident occurred while I was patrolling in the North Woods. Maine State Police had a field office in Guilford at the Public Works Department. It was a little room where we kept supplies and a desk and did reports. We also manned it a few hours each week, so people could come in and get permits or whatever.

One early evening while I was at the office, a person stopped by to report an accident just happened downtown near the IGA. I closed up the office and headed to the scene.

People stood around a parked vehicle next to the sidewalk. The rear of the vehicle was completely demolished. Witnesses said a person driving an older green Dodge had run into the back of the parked car and taken off toward Abbot. It all happened in just the previous few minutes.

I told the bystanders to stay put and I would try to catch up with the suspect vehicle. I quickly took off toward Abbot, and didn't have to go far.

As I left the built-up portion of Guilford, almost in front of the senior citizen homes, an old green Dodge was stopped in the middle of the road. I pulled in behind it and turned on the blue lights. As I got out of my cruiser and approached the green Dodge, I could see an elderly gentleman walking in front of his car.

I asked him, "What are you doing?"

"I'm looking for my driveway," he blurted out.

"You're looking for what?" I asked in disbelief.

"My driveway!"

That is when I noticed the front of his vehicle. It was completely smashed. One headlight was shattered and the other headlight hung by its wires. It still worked and lit the ground. This was obviously the car that had just struck the parked vehicle in town.

"Do you know you just ran into a parked car down by the IGA?" I asked him.

"You know, I wondered why my groceries fell on the floor," he told me.

I couldn't help but chuckle; he had a great sense of humor and made fun of his situation. He went on to tell me he wasn't supposed to be driving after dark, as he couldn't see. But his grocery shopping took a little longer than expected and when he came out of the store, it was already dark. So he tried to drive the short distance home.

I got the accident taken care of and made sure the man got his groceries and himself into his home for the night. I felt badly for him, as I knew after my report was received by the Secretary of State that the man would probably lose his license and therefore that last bit of independence.

Just another day in the life of a trooper.

Saved by a Seatbelt

The following domestic violence incident was extremely dangerous and ended with a permanent solution to a temporary problem.

It involved my dear friend, Maxim "Mickey" Squiers, chief of the Greenville Police Department. He was nearing the end of his career and looking forward to a lengthy, quiet retirement.

I dealt with a similar situation that involved the death of two people. When it was all over, I could only imagine what was going through the minds of those involved.

This particular couple had gotten together under perhaps the most unscrupulous method. Both were married to other people and after long sordid details, eventually they ended up as a couple. The road was rocky and there were many problems. The male was eventually ordered to leave the residence and he was not legally allowed to return. The female soon found romance elsewhere and the man was going insane seeing the woman have another male visitor.

When the man drove by the woman's home, which he was not allowed to do, the woman called the police. The police in this small town consisted of Mickey.

Each time Mickey caught the man. It is fair to say Mickey spent many hours talking with this man about the situation. This man did not like that the woman was moving on and it was going to be without him.

It was also fair to say Mickey was getting tired of dealing with this same situation over and over.

One day a call came in for assistance. The man was at his former girlfriend's workplace and he was running through the building with a shotgun trying to find her. Mickey arrived first at the scene. Backup was on the way.

When Mickey made his way into the workplace, the man saw him and made a desperate attempt to escape. Mickey corralled the man back at his vehicle without anyone getting injured. However, a major confrontation took place there and Mickey was held at bay at the end of the man's shotgun.

After talking with this man for a short period of time, it was obvious he had gone to the business to kill the woman and then himself. While being held at gunpoint, Mickey was negotiating and trying to bring the incident to a peaceful conclusion.

Assistance arrived in the form of a local warden. "Whoa!" was the word Maine Warden Lt. Dorian mustered as he rounded the corner of the pickup and saw Mickey at the end of the gun barrel.

The man, totally frustrated he couldn't do what he set out to do, decided to make a run for it in his pickup. He screeched out of the parking lot and headed north toward Rockwood.

Mickey got behind the fleeing vehicle and snapped on his seat belt, expecting a high-speed chase to ensue.

Just as they rounded the turn in Greenville Junction in front of Breton's Store, there was a tractor-trailer truck making a delivery and blocking the entire road. The man on the run had just run out of room.

When Mickey went to get out of his vehicle he got hung up in his seat belt. Adrenalin pumping, it took him a couple of seconds to untangle the seat belt, exit his cruiser and approach the suspect.

As Mickey told me later, at that point he was so angry with the man he was going to rip him out of the truck and make him stop this whole foolish behavior. Mickey knew the man quite well.

Mickey worked his way out of his cruiser and approached the pickup. When he got to the door, he reached for the handle. A loud explosion sounded and Mickey felt something strike his arm.

Mickey opened the door and looked in. The suspect had blown his head completely off. There was nothing left of the man above his shoulders. Pieces of the suspect had struck Mickey's arm. Mickey was dumbfounded and speechless. There was nothing he could do.

One second this man was alive and then he was dead.

That day, the seat belt actually saved Mickey's life. If he had not gotten tangled up in it and had exited the vehicle a few seconds earlier, he might have been in the direct line of fire and been shot.

Seeing this happen right in front of his eyes was devastating for the veteran officer. It's something he carried for the rest of his life, not just to the end of his career.

I recently took Mickey and his lovely wife, Simone, to dinner and Mickey retold this story just as if it happened yesterday. And this horrific incident took place in the early 1990s.

To look at the positive side, Mickey saved the life of the estranged girlfriend. After the investigation, it was clear the suspect's intent that day was to murder her then commit suicide.

Just another day in the life of a police officer.

Speaking from the Grave

This story is about a dear friend who passed away at a young age while fighting a fire and trying to save lives. I miss him a lot. His name is Robert Jones, or "Jonesy" as everyone called him.

We are nearing the anniversary of his death, which was also his birthday, and I think of him often.

I first met Jonesy in 1982, when I transferred to Unity from the Moosehead Lake Region. For five hours each day, he worked at the Unity Hardware Store, then he worked nights at the Waldo County Sheriff's Department as a deputy.

The hardware store became known as the Waldo County Sheriff's substation—in other words, Jonesy's little office during the day when he was supposed to be off-duty.

Many people went to the hardware store for law enforcement purposes as well as to shop for tools. I immediately took a liking to Jonesy and spent many hours talking with him and learning about local people. He knew everyone and was admired by most.

No matter what I asked of Jonesy, he never said no to any request. I often wondered how he got so much done. I learned a great deal from him about the importance of family. He loved his daughters more than anything and talked about them a lot.

One quality I admired about Jonesy was his capacity to reach out and help people. He went the extra mile to assist the less fortunate and young kids leaning toward trouble. He tried to smooth things over, resolve issues and keep in touch with troubled teens so he could steer them in the right direction.

It took a lot of his time but he did it willingly and never grumbled. I could go on and on about Jonesy, but I want to share this story with you to show how he actually spoke from the grave to one young man whom he helped when he was alive.

I got a call late one afternoon from the Waldo County Sheriff's office requesting assistance. There was a young, out-of-control male in Burnham tearing up a house. No deputies were in the area, and I was the closest trooper.

I made my way over to Burnham, pulled into the yard of the residence and turned my cruiser so it pointed right at the wide-open front door of the trailer. Just inside was the out-of-control young man. I could see him thrashing around; he was clearly drunk and barely able to stand.

He turned, looked out the front door and saw my cruiser. He looked like a deer caught in headlights—staring at my cruiser and not moving. I jumped out and started into the trailer. He saw that I was after him and quickly ran down the hallway of the trailer into the last bedroom, with me right behind him.

I was not quick enough to grab him before he got to the other side of the king-size bed, just out of my reach. However, at least he was corralled and could no longer hurt anyone or damage anything.

So there we were in a standoff in the bedroom. I told him to calm down and we would take care of whatever it was that was bothering him. He was highly agitated and wasn't in too much of a mood to calm down or even talk with me. No matter what I did or said, it didn't seem to matter. I knew that I was going to have to get physical with him to take him into custody.

Then I remembered. This young man was someone whom Jonesy had once reached out to and tried to help. Under Jonesy's help, this young man actually did quite well and kept out of trouble. I decided to speak with him about Jonesy.

"What would Jonesy think right now if he was here with us," I asked Jamie.

Jamie looked at me as though he was filled with hatred. But as soon as I mentioned Jonesy's name, it hit him. All the hatred left his face, and he broke down and cried. Everything changed right then and there, and we talked for quite some time.

He walked around the bed and gave himself up. I had to take him to jail, but I told him that Jonesy would be proud that he made the right decision and didn't make matters worse. It actually was an enjoyable ride as we spoke about our mutual friend all the way to jail. Thank you, Jonesy!

Just another day in the life of a trooper.

Oh No, Not You Again!

Perhaps my greatest accomplishment as a state trooper was removing a large number of drunk drivers from our highways.

Even though the situation was dire, many drunks were humorous to deal with and very entertaining. I always dealt with the suspects respectfully, realizing that most had made a bad judgment call by getting behind the wheel after drinking too much.

Even though some were hardcore drunks and hard to deal with, it made me feel good to get these people off our highways before they killed themselves or an innocent motorist.

I thought I would share a couple of stories about two different people with whom I interacted. Both were arrested many times for drunk driving.

The first fellow I ran across in the parking lot at Squaw Mountain Ski Resort in the Moosehead Lake region. It was early one winter evening and as I entered the parking lot, I observed several people attempting to push a Saab out of a snow bank.

I drove over to where they were and got out to assist. After the vehicle was out of the snow bank, I approached the operator and noticed he was absolutely smashed.

He told me he had been driving and somehow lost control and went into the snow bank. After he produced his driver's license, I recognized his name from a well-to-do family from the Augusta area.

I told him about the problem he was in, not that he had gone off the road, but that he was driving while drunk. I told him we had to go through the OUI process and I would be charging him with OUI.

He was very cooperative and accepted it was going to happen. He also told me this was the first time he had ever dealt with a state trooper and thanked me for being kind. This happened in the late '70s in Piscataquis County.

In the mid-'80s, I was patrolling near a bar on Route 3 in Liberty. Soon after the bar closed, I observed a small pickup being driven poorly and I made a traffic stop. As I approached the operator and asked for his license, he looked at me and said, "Hi Mark."

I looked at him very closely and finally recognized him from the Squaw Mountain incident. All I could say was, "You're kidding me!"

"Nope, it's me. And yes, I'm drunk again."

"That you are, without a doubt," I told him and once again put him through the OUI process. I then made arrangements for his vehicle to be driven home and I took him home.

We talked all the way to his house about the fact that this was the second time that he ever had contact with a state trooper and it was for OUI once again. He joked he hoped he never ever saw me again on the road and for me to not stop him. Even though it was comical, it really wasn't. This incident took place in the mid-'80s in Liberty in Waldo County.

Now onto the late '90s. I was running radar on Route 3 in South China and clocked a full-size van traveling eastbound. It was going 73 mph and I flipped around to make a stop on the van. Again, as I approached the operator, he rolled his window down and all I heard was, "Oh no, it can't be you again!"

I looked at the driver and sure enough, there was old Clyde. Not only was he speeding, but he was again drunk.

"Aren't you tired of me yet," I asked him.

"You bet I am. Three times I've been stopped, all by you and this is the third OUI that I have gotten. How do you keep catching me?" he asked.

"Well, you're just a good guy, and I hadn't seen you for quite awhile and thought I would say 'hi,'" I told him.

Clyde got a chuckle from the comment and I again drove him home after putting him through the OUI process. He had aged quite a bit from the first time I ran into him back in the '70s. He told me that he thought that he might just as well give up driving as he was getting too old to deal with me for the rest of his life.

To make this story even more unbelievable was the fact that in the new millennium, just before I retired, I was called to a motor-vehicle crash in Windsor, and the driver was none other than Clyde's brother.

Once he learned who I was, I could hear him mutter, "Uh-oh." He too was processed for OUI and we chatted about his brother, particularly that I had not seen his brother during the decade.

The other fellow I want to tell you about is a young man I knew in the Guilford area. He worked in an auto parts store and was a pretty good kid. I liked cars and often we talked cars while I was in the store getting parts.

Then one night while patrolling in the Guilford area, I made a traffic stop on a vehicle that I suspected for OUI. The driver turned out to be the young man from the auto parts store and, yes, he was drunk.

Turns out he wasn't so nice when drinking, and he started to give me a difficult time. And because he was being difficult with me, his vehicle got towed and he got transported to the county jail in Dover-Foxcroft. It was around 10 p.m. when I finally cleared the arrest. I went back out on patrol and drove north to Greenville.

It was about 1:30 a.m. when I came upon another vehicle that needed to be stopped due to its poor operation. I pulled over the car and approached the operator.

I could not believe my eyes when I observed the same young man from the auto parts store driving this vehicle as well. And he was even more snookered than when I stopped him earlier in the evening.

The young man kept telling me, "Man you're good. Man you're good."

"What are you talking about anyway?" I asked him.

"You get me in Guilford at 10 p.m. driving my car. It is now 1:30 a.m., I'm 30 miles away and driving a different car and you caught me again. Now that's good," he said.

I thanked him for his compliment and again processed him for the OUI, towed his vehicle and took him to jail. This time I asked them to try and keep him behind bars for the rest of the night. It would be pathetic to get the same person three times in one night.

Thinking back, it really was something to get one person for OUI three times, in three different decades, in three different vehicles, in three different counties.

Not to mention to catch a young man twice in one shift, within a 30-mile range in two different vehicles.

Either that or incredibly bad luck on their part.

Oh well, just another day in the life.

Getting Comfortable

The last thing I remembered before drifting off early in the morning was that I could sleep in. I was certainly looking forward to not having to be anywhere and getting caught up on some long-overdue beauty rest.

It wasn't meant to be. I heard a ringing noise during a wonderful dream. It took a while for it to register that it was the phone.

"Hello," I answered in a raspy voice.

"Mark?"

"Yes," I answered.

"This is Roger. Do you know if the Broadway Furniture store in Bangor was broken into last night?" he asked.

Roger owned and operated a local wrecker service in the Waldo County area. He was also my neighbor.

"I haven't got a clue, besides that is in a different zone and I wouldn't get that information until the teletypes came out," I told him.

"Well, I think I heard on the scanner that the store was broken into and, if that is true, I may have some information for you."

"What have you got, Roger?" I asked, not wanting to completely wake up. I kept my eyes closed while speaking with him.

"I got a call in the night of a truck stuck in a ditch and they just needed a tow to get it out. So I went to the location and there was a Broadway Furniture truck with one wheel stuck in a ditch. There wasn't any damage so I didn't call the police," he said. "So I hooked onto the truck, pulled it out of the ditch and got it on its way."

I hated to ask the next question because I always seemed to get an answer that I dreaded.

"Did you know who the driver was or who had control of the vehicle?" I finally got the courage to ask, while wincing at the same time.

"Yes I do," Roger told me.

Well, that got my interest and I finally opened my eyes, knowing that this might turn out to be something. "Well, who was it?" I asked.

"It was Tommy Smith, and it just didn't seem right at the time." he replied.

"Really."

I knew Tommy quite well and knew he had already pulled a serious theft once before and made off with quite a haul before getting caught.

I told Roger to stay put, and I would get back to him.

I called the Bangor Police Department and spoke with dispatch and inquired whether the Broadway Furniture store had recently been broken into.

"Why, yes it was. Just last night, and we have two detectives at the store as we speak doing a crime scene. I can forward your phone call through to them if you would like."

"Sure."

Soon enough, I was speaking with one of the detectives at the store. He confirmed the store was, in fact, broken into and they were actively investigating and processing the crime scene. I asked him if one of the delivery trucks was missing.

"Yes, it looks like they loaded up one of the trucks with furniture from the store, opened the door and drove off. And they took the expensive stuff, lots of it, a whole truck load of it," the detective said.

"Any leads yet?" I asked.

"Not yet, but we should know more after we get done here."

I told them that I would get back to them soon about some information I had received that morning.

My neighbor seemed to have the key to solve the crime. I called Roger and got all of his details—the time it happened, exactly where it was and who was around when it occurred. Then I got suited up and headed to work.

I landed at Tommy's house first thing. His car was not there when I knocked on the front door. No answer. As I turned to go back to my cruiser, Tommy pulled into the driveway. He got out of his car and approached me as I walked back to my cruiser.

Tommy is a very cool person. He never let on that something was up. He acted very calm and asked me if I needed anything.

"Yes, Tommy, I need that Broadway Furniture truck that you have."

I don't think Tommy was expecting such a blunt comment. He looked at me like I was stupid. "I have no idea what you're talking about," he said.

"OK Tommy, let's not play any games. The game is over, and I know you have the furniture truck. You can cooperate or not, it does not matter to me," I told him.

Tommy studied me for a long time. I knew him well enough that he was not going to 'fess up to anything unless I had him really good. "So what makes you think I have the truck?" he asked.

"Were you stuck in a ditch with it last night?" I asked. As I watched his facial expression, I knew he knew that I knew. His face turned from defiant to looking like a kid who got his hand caught in the cookie jar.

"You know, I haven't been to sleep all night. That was a big job. Loading up a truck full of good furniture, driving down here and then unloading it and trying to find a good hiding place," he told me.

"Well, where is it now?" I asked him.

"You'll never find it. I'll take you."

"No, I'll take you and you can show me." I said, chuckling.

Tommy got in my cruiser and we headed for Knox. As we were traveling along Route 137 near Sanborn Pond, Tommy told me to turn onto a little trail that went into a field. Parked right in the middle of the field was the Broadway Furniture truck. The rear doors were open and grandfather clocks, recliners, couches, chairs, tables and much more were all in the field.

"So what was your plan after all this?" I asked.

"Well, the first thing was to get some sleep. Then I was going to call some friends and have a furniture sale out here in the field."

"You're kidding me, right?"

"Nope, that was the plan, except you got in the way," he said.

I drove to the store in Waldo and called the Bangor PD to speak with the detectives. I asked them if they would like the truck and all the furniture back.

"You mean you got it," they asked.

"Yes, it's here in Knox. And you can come and get it."

After I gave them directions, they headed my way. I showed them the truck and the makeshift, open-air furniture store that Tommy had assembled in the middle of the field. The detectives were grateful. They inventoried the items and took photos of the scene. One of the detectives was a cigar smoker and I could not resist having a little fun with the whole matter.

One of the very few times I ever put on my Stetson was for this occasion. I asked a Bangor detective if he would take my photo with the recovered loot. I put on my Stetson, took his cigar and sprawled out in one of the nice recliners in the middle of the field while he snapped some pictures of the occasion.

I had to say, whenever Tommy did a crime, he certainly knew how to do it big time.

After the loot was loaded back into the truck and was on its way to Bangor, I went home and got some of that much-needed sleep.

Just another day in the life.

Murder in the North Woods

I'll start this story by saying that not everything in the career of a trooper is fun. Perhaps about a quarter of the incidents are sprinkled with humor.

It is unbelievable how people get themselves into precarious situations. A lot laugh at their predicaments, chalk them up as a lesson well learned, and make sure it's not repeated.

I know a lot of officers who dealt with the harsh reality of the job by trying to find humor in situations. I was certainly one of those.

But let's face it, sometimes there isn't any humor in a predicament. Sometimes the situations are devastating, like helping retrieve the bodies of three boys who perished in a home fire. And telling a mother that her son was killed in a motor vehicle crash. You just deal with it the best way you can.

This particular incident happened early in my career. I learned several valuable lessons from it. One was to be careful of what I said because words could later come back to haunt me. That was certainly the case in this story.

I realized that wearing the uniform of a Maine State Police trooper was a responsibility. People looked at me for guidance and assistance and it was my job to provide that and a whole lot more.

I need to tell you about the work schedule required of troopers at the time. When I came on in 1977, the schedule was six days a week, 24 hours a day. We were required to put in a minimum of 10 hours patrol on the road. The report writing, cruiser cleaning, taking care of the gear and all other parts of the job were outside of that 10 hours.

Even at home, we were expected to be ready as soon as the phone rang to respond to any and all calls.

There was no overtime and my monthly time sheet ran between 350 to 400 hours. If court fell on your day off, too bad. I have to admit, though, it was a very exciting job as I was young and could not get enough. I wanted to go all the time. But for guys with families, it was extremely tough.

This past year, I talked with the person who committed the crime I am about to share. He was interested in knowing how I was, as he had heard I had retired. We talked by phone and I stopped in to see him. I could almost see his eyes well up with tears as we sat down to talk. We filled each other in on our lives for the prior 25 years or so.

When I told him that I wrote stories, I could tell he was interested in knowing more. I mentioned I would like to tell his story, as well. He said, "Please do, Mark." So here goes.

It was Dec. 3, 1979, when I got my first call from Maurietta O'Brien. She and her husband, Bob, lived in an old farmhouse on the outskirts of Monson. It was a beautiful old farmhouse, with several large attached and unattached barns. The scenery, which was mostly mountains, was almost 360 degrees.

The fields were open and tended. Bob had a collection of old Thunderbirds from the '50s and '60s and a few Mustangs from the same era. I loved old cars, particularly Thunderbirds. I had learned from locals that his barns were full of these cars and parts and he had more in the fields that could not be seen from the road.

Before this night, I had never met Bob and his wife, Maurietta. There was a good reason for this. I had learned he was from away and he was a long-haul trucker. But he was nearing retirement and he wanted to go north and live in a quiet place, choosing Monson, Maine to be it.

Bob had only been around a short period of time and did not know many people. Unfortunately for him, one local who befriended him was perhaps one of the worst criminals in the area. Bob didn't realize this until it was too late. Of course, when the locals saw who he hung around with, not many wanted much to do with him. As nice as he was, Bob earned a bad reputation.

As for the guy he hung with—words cannot describe what a mean-spirited person he was. I knew his reputation and record very well. It was long and went back many years.

The call from Mauri came in to me at about 9 p.m. As soon as I finished with a drunk driver whom I had arrested, I headed to Mauri's house from Skowhegan. The initial call was about a theft.

However after my arrival, it was certainly more than a theft. After being invited into the home, we sat down at the dining room table. Bob asked me if I had time to listen to the whole story. I got out my notebook and told Bob that I had all the time he needed.

As Bob started his story, I could see the worried look on his face. This man and his wife were living in fear of what might happen to them for talking to me.

Bob said he had wanted to move to the area and retire. He thought he found the perfect place and subsequently bought and moved into the farmhouse.

One of the first people to come around was "Al." Being new to the area, Bob did not realize who Al was. Al hung around more and more and soon the two were pretty good friends. But as time went on, Bob realized Al liked trouble. Not only did he make a lot of trouble for people, but anyone who crossed Al lived to regret it.

I will give you an example of what Al was like.

An elderly lady who lived near Bob had water pump problems. Al was a handyman and the lady contacted him and asked him if he could fix her water problem. Al told her he could fix it and gave her a cost estimate. The elderly lady told Al that she did not have that kind of money but she could make monthly payments until it was paid off.

They reached an agreement and Al said he would do the work. Once the work was done, the elderly lady kept her end of the deal by making the monthly payments.

However, after a short period of time, Al changed his mind and wanted all the money in one lump sum. He approached the elderly lady and demanded his money. She said she did not have the money but would continue to pay as they had agreed. That did not sit well with Al so one night he got a five-gallon can of diesel fuel and dumped it in her well, destroying her water supply.

Bob started to tell me other things that Al had done. I was familiar with some of them and had worked on the cases. Al was always the suspect but we never had enough to charge him with the crimes. A majority of the crimes were felonies and if we could convict Al, he would probably spend the remainder of his years in the slammer.

I was amazed at Bob's detailed stories. He had the inside track on Al and knew just about everything the man had done for the last couple of years. We talked and talked. Finally, Bob got to his point. He was afraid and he wanted to break off his friendship with Al.

However, Bob realized he knew too much about him and that Al would not allow them to stop being friends. And if it happened, Al would retaliate. Bob's biggest concern was his family, then his property. He knew Al had committed arson and Bob had those barns full of T-birds and car parts.

Then came the barrage of questions. "Do I have the right to protect my life and my property?" Bob asked me. "What would happen to me if I shot him while he was setting fire to my property?"

As an off-the-cuff remark, I told Bob the town would probably pin a medal on him if he shot Al. I clearly didn't mean it seriously; it was a wise remark.

Later, I would come to eat those words and they went down very hard. And I did tell Bob that he had the right to protect him and his family if they felt they were in threat of imminent danger.

We continued talking for many hours. It finally came down to this. I would patrol his property as often as I could. What I needed from Bob were written statements pertaining to what he knew about Al's criminal activities. Then we could go after Al.

At that time, Bob was not willing to do this but he said he would think about it. After several hours of talking, I left the Monson farmhouse, quite worried about Bob and Mauri. But I was hopeful that Bob would give me what I needed to bring charges against the area's most notorious criminal.

Next time, the conclusion of this sad story.

Murder in the North Woods
Part II

Leaving the old farmhouse, I was very concerned for Bob and Mauri's safety. I knew who they were up against and it was going to be a battle.

Bob was going to have many sleepless nights worrying about his barns being burned and wondering what Al might do to them and when he might do it.

I assured them I would do all I could do and would patrol around their home as often as possible. Whether this made them feel any better, I was not sure but they seemed happy whenever I hung around.

Bob severed all ties with Al. When this happened, it was like going on high alert. I spent every free moment when not tied up on other cases, constantly checking Bob's home and checking on Al's whereabouts.

I would go by Bob's house sometimes at 3 or 4 a.m. and see a flashlight shining around his barns. It always turned out to be Bob and we would check his property together. Many times, Bob would get into my cruiser and we would talk through the night. During the ordeal we became friends.

Bob, of course, knew what I was encouraging him to do. I wanted him to give written statements pertaining to all of Al's criminal activities he knew about. It was always part of our conversation and I thought he was starting to lean that way.

I continued patrolling Bob's property and kept in touch with Bob and Mauri. I stepped it up so I could be seen near his property by as many people, including Al, as possible. One night, the patrolling paid off.

I drove into the area very late at night and when I got near the old farmhouse, I shut off the cruiser's headlights and slowly drove by Bob's home.

And there he was. Al was parked just beyond the farmhouse, taking up nearly all the driving lane, with his vehicle running, and all his lights off.

I could tell there was one person who was smoking and flicking ashes out the window. I stopped and watched. I was sure Al might do something and I was in the perfect place to catch him. I waited and waited. He just sat there. I told myself I could outwait him no matter what. It was exciting to think what this guy might try to do and I had a chance to catch him right in the act.

As it turned out, time was not on my side. I received a call from Maine State Police Augusta to respond to a call. In those days, there were no pagers and no cell phones and I had to find a payphone. But I definitely wasn't going to leave without Al knowing that I was right there with him.

I inched in behind Al's truck and, all at once, turned on my headlights and my blue lights. I jumped out of the cruiser and approached Al, who was sitting behind the wheel of the pickup. Even though I knew I startled him, he tried to act as cool as he could and look like nothing was up. I asked him what he was doing there so late at night.

His reply: "None of your business."

"Well it is my business when you park in the roadway, in front of someone else's home and you have no business to be here," I replied.

"I'll do whatever I want to do and you can't do anything about it," he defiantly said.

I knew Al was one to watch and was careful around him. I checked him over and spied everything else I could see from my vantage point. Maybe he was there to see what might happen if he hung around, maybe he was checking the security and to see if he would be discovered. Maybe he had material to set a fire. But one thing was for sure, he knew the police were watching him very closely.

I told Al he needed to move on. He looked right at me and said, "I don't have to do anything you tell me to do."

"If you don't move along, Al, I will tow your truck," I warned him.

"You have no right to do that," Al replied.

"You are parked in the driving lane and impeding traffic. I have every right to keep the roadway open and safe," I threw right back at him.

"Show me in the law book," he said, still being defiant.

"The only thing I am going to show you is me calling a tow truck on my radio. Now leave," I said, a lot more forceful than before.

Reluctantly, Al put his truck in gear and drove away.

The situation was clearly in the open between Bob, Mauri, Al and local law enforcement. I kept watching Bob's property, kept in touch with Bob and pressured him for those statements. I thought for sure the only way this whole situation would go away would be to get enough on

Al to arrest him for the felonies he had committed over the years. He would then be in jail and Bob and his wife could live in peace.

This whole incident had started Dec. 3, 1979. On Saturday Dec. 29, I spent several hours checking and watching Bob's property. At 4 p.m., I talked with Bob, and at 2:20 a.m. Dec. 30, I watched his property. I signed off at home at 4:25 a.m. Sunday in Greenville Junction.

At 10 a.m. Sunday, the ringing phone woke me up. It was Bob. He said he had weighed it over and that he was ready to provide statements, after which I would be able to charge Al. I remember telling Bob that he would not regret his decision. I would be at his home later that day and we would start the process. I hung up the phone feeling very good but tired. I went right back to sleep. At 12:30 p.m., the phone rang again.

"Mark? This is Bob, I just shot the son of a bitch!"

"You what?"

"I shot him."

"Is he dead?" I asked.

"Yes."

"Don't do anything Bob, I'll be right there!"

My mind raced as I got up, dressed, jumped in the cruiser and headed to Bob's house. Maine State Police in Augusta had been notified of the incident and other appropriate personnel were on their way as well.

I arrived at the old farmhouse and met Bob. He came out of his home and got into the cruiser. On Bob's property was a small two-room cabin that he rented. The building was no more than 12 feet by 16 feet with a woodstove in the front room. The cabin was near the road on the corner of Bob's front lawn. Apparently, the renter had company over that morning and the person was an acquaintance of Al. Bob saw Al arrive on his property and go into the cabin. Bob thought the only reason Al was there was to aggravate him.

O'Brien cabin

Bob was extremely nervous. He got his rifle and went over to the cabin. He wanted to find out why Al was there and to tell him to leave. Al was defiant—a big mistake on his part. Bob, fearing for his life, lowered the gun and pulled the trigger. Al was dead before he hit the floor.

I checked the body. Sure enough, Al was dead. There were two witnesses. One of them, David, a local drunk from Greenville, was still seated on the couch, his blue eyes as wide as saucers. He didn't dare move and hadn't moved since it happened almost a half hour before. It was obvious

David was quite happy to see me that day, unlike all the other times I dealt with him. I briefly spoke to each of them and told them to stay put as a detective from the Maine State Police would be taking their statements.

It wasn't long before the detectives arrived and took over the crime scene. It was my introduction to Detective Rexford Kelley and Detective Bruce Rafnell. The criminal division of the Maine State Police investigates all homicides in Maine, except for in Portland and Bangor.

I introduced Bob to Detective Kelley and encouraged Bob to tell him the whole story. It was the only way for the detectives to understand what type of situation Bob and his wife had been living in due to Al. I placed Bob in Detective Kelley's cruiser and we traveled to the Maine State Police field office in Guilford for an interview.

I could tell Detective Kelley was a great interviewer. Bob talked with him at ease and told him the story from the beginning. The problem was we never reached the end. Bob's wife, Mauri, arrived and told Bob to stop talking. She had hired an attorney and he had sent word for Bob to stop talking. To me, this was the worst thing that could have happened. Detective Kelley had no choice but to arrest Bob for the murder of Al.

I provided written statements to Detective Kelley of all my contacts with the case over the past month. It was then, when it became evident that I had said something earlier that was definitely going to come back and bite me. My statement, "The town will probably pin a medal on you" after Bob asked what would happen if he shot Al, loomed large. I will never forget Detective Kelley's reaction when he saw that statement. "You said what?!"

The trial:

Bob had the support of the public, myself included, even though I could not say it aloud. As a trooper, I was to remain neutral and not express my feelings. Sometimes this was tough to do, but it had to be done and I understood why.

I was hoping for a lesser plea of manslaughter but the AG's office prosecuted for murder. The defense lawyer's best chance of getting at the truth was through me, as most lawyers will not put defendants on the stand to testify.

I remember being on the stand—I was there for one reason and that was to tell the truth about the whole story, no matter what. I got through the prosecutor's questions without any problems and then it was the defense attorney's turn.

In my opinion, this guy should not have been badgering me. But he was trying to make points and his questions were more like statements. It got so bad at one point I stopped listening to his tirade. When he was done I simply said, "Could you repeat that?"

I think I made him very angry and he wanted to make me look bad. Then my statement came up about the "town pinning a medal on Bob."

I replied, "Well, the crime rate did drop after the shooting."

The courtroom erupted and the judge explained the remark would be stricken from the record. To this day, I still believe I told it like it was.

About midway through the trial, the State allowed Bob to plead to manslaughter and he received eight years in prison for shooting Al.

Bob went to jail. He left the retirement home for which he had worked most of his life. He left his wife, Mauri, to fend for herself. She died not too many years later.

Today, Bob still has his old farmhouse and most of the old Thunderbirds are in the barns. And he is trying to live a quiet normal life just like he tried to 30 years ago.

Just another day in the life.

The One Time I Almost Lost It

I always prided myself on having a strong stomach and not letting much bother me. The things I saw as a trooper would have sent most people over the edge.

I have no idea why I could stand the most gruesome scenes but, for the most part, they never bothered me. I did, however, try to imagine what had been going through their mind just prior to their demise. If only a few circumstances had been different, who knows, the end might not have come so soon.

My dad, who was a retired captain of the Maine State Police and in charge of the homicide bureau, had given me good advice. He warned me about things that I would see and autopsies that I would be attending. He gave me hints on how to deal with such things and, believe me, his advice came in handy many times.

I will never forget one late fall when a person was reported missing. An extensive investigation was done and the person seemed to have just vanished. Early in the spring, the missing person's vehicle was seen by a bystander standing on a bridge watching the spring runoff.

I responded and after seeing the vehicle in the water, called for a wrecker. Eventually, the vehicle was pulled from the water. After most of the water had drained from the vehicle, I opened the passenger door and there indeed was the missing person we had been looking for since fall. The wrecker operator, who seemed so brave and wanted to assist in any way he could, took one look and immediately went to his knees vomiting. For some reason, it just never bothered me in that way. I was saddened that such a young person had lost his life in a terrible way though.

So I thought I would share with you the one time I did almost lose it.

There was a particular bar in Abbott that troopers worked pretty hard weekend nights. It seemed as though drinkers never got the hint that they could drink all they wanted, and they could drive all they wanted—just not at the same time.

It's pretty simple. If you're going to drink, don't drive. If you're going to drive, don't drink. However this particular bar supplied an unlimited number of drunk drivers for our highways and it was my duty to remove them as quickly as I could.

This one particular night was no different. I had luck patrolling the area rather than sitting still and watching the traffic. Driving north and south of the bar on Route 15, I went by the saloon heading south and into Guilford. It was about closing time and patrons were pouring out. I would follow some of the patrons as they left and observe their driving habits. Having no reason to stop them, I would turn back toward the bar to meet more traffic.

That is when I got a call that there was an accident with serious personal injury on Route 15 in Guilford about two miles south of the bar— it must have happened right behind me. I raced back to the scene, arriving about the same time as the ambulance.

After traveling a short distance in a straight line, a four-door Subaru had gone straight off the road; the driver had not even attempted the right turn and had struck a utility pole dead front center of the Subaru.

There were five passengers in the vehicle—four young ladies and one young man. The women were seated in each corner of the vehicle, wearing seat belts, while the young man was seated in the middle of the back seat and was not wearing a seat belt.

The front had bucket seats. When the vehicle struck the pole and hence came to an abrupt stop, he was catapulted headfirst from the back seat, through the windshield and into the utility pole.

When I approached, the young man was sitting on the ground leaning against a tree a few feet from the pole. Blood was pouring from his head all over his clothes. I thought for sure he was dead or was going to be soon.

The young man spoke. "Mark, it's me, Terry. And guess what? I wasn't driving," he said. He was clearly very happy with himself that he had chose to ride instead of drive, as he was feeling no pain.

I still had a difficult time identifying him. "Are you OK?" I asked.

"Oh yeah. I feel fine." He then grabbed his forehead and literally pushed his face back up.

I was flabbergasted. Apparently when he went through the windshield and struck the utility pole, he cut his scalp from one ear, over the top of his head and down to the other ear. His scalp had slid down his face and the back of his head. Once he had pulled his "face" back up I could tell who he was.

"This is what you get when you do things the right way, Terry?" I asked.

I had many run-ins with Terry over a short period of time. He had lost his license due to drinking and driving and I always seemed to be the one to catch him. He wasn't a bad kid, it just took him awhile to figure out to stop driving when he was drinking.

"Go figure. Good thing I drank a lot tonight, huh, Mark?"

"Well, if you can't feel anything, I would say that is a good thing for you right now. But we have to get you in the ambulance and take you to the hospital so they can stitch your scalp back on."

"OK," he said, very willing to cooperate.

Terry was transported to the hospital while I finished cleaning up at the scene, charging the driver with drunk driving and issuing summonses. After clearing the scene, I headed to the hospital to check on Terry and get a statement.

I arrived at the hospital and was escorted into one of the ER rooms, where the doctor was starting to treat Terry. I was told of the extent of his injuries—the X-rays proved his skull did not fracture and all he needed was to have his scalp stitched back up.

I arrived just as the doctor was injecting Novocain into his scalp. Up to that point, I had done fine. But watching the needles, then the clips being put on his scalp to hold it in place while the doctor started sewing, and the smell of the hospital...well, that was enough for me.

It hit suddenly. My knees went weak, I became lightheaded and the room started to spin. I was in trouble and needed to do something quickly so I didn't look like I was wimping out in the hospital.

I immediately stopped looking at Terry and sat down on a stool. I put my head down and swallowed to keep everything down. I pretended to be writing Terry's statement in my notebook. Thankfully, no one seemed to be the wiser, as they were all busy anyway. After a short time, I stepped outside, got a breath of fresh air, which brought me back to normal.

Terry recovered nicely from his injury and I never picked him up again for OUI. And that was the one time I almost lost it.

Just another day in the life.

Pardon Me

It was a lovely warm spring day in the North Country. People had been cooped up all winter and finally a day arrived when everyone wanted to be outside enjoying the beautiful, sunny, warm weather.

As I patrolled the different towns, I saw people outside cleaning their yards and playing with their children.

I had just gone through Guilford into Abbot and was heading north toward Monson when Maine State Police HQ alerted me of a property-damage motor-vehicle crash in Guilford.

It must have happened right after I went through town. I turned around, put on my blue lights and headed back to Guilford.

At the Abbot/Guilford town line, I came up behind two motorcycles traveling side by side probably 10 to 15 miles over the speed limit. Not having time to stop them, I got closer so they would notice me and pull over to let me by.

Funny how things never work out the way you want them to, or the way you think they might.

The motorcyclist on the right looked back, noticed me and motioned to his friend to pull over. The motorcyclist on the right pulled over, but the one on the left looked back, turned back around, leaned down and took off at a blistering rate of speed.

Oh, this is just great, I thought to myself.

So the chase was on, right into Guilford.

It was a busy Saturday morning and I was on the tail of this motorcycle, blue lights flashing and siren wailing, hoping the biker would stop. But no luck. He kept going, zigzagging through downtown traffic. He picked spots and places that he thought I could not get through, but I simply followed him. Although once, my rear bumper nicked the bumper of a car as I squeezed through a particularly tight spot on a bridge.

We even went by the accident scene that I had been called to earlier. I can't imagine what those people were thinking as I blew by them with lights and siren on.

All I could do while they tried to flag me down was sort of put my hand up, trying to signal that I would be back in a minute or so.

The bike was a crotch rocket that had plenty of speed and acceleration. I was doing my best to stay with it and, in all honesty, was doing quite well. We had made it through the built-up portion of Guilford and I could tell the cyclist was getting ready to make a left turn onto Route 150 just east of town.

The biker made some wild maneuvers. I knew he was going way too fast to make the turn and, sure enough, down he went. The bike slid across the pavement, over the sidewalk and onto a residential lawn.

It didn't come to a stop until he reached the driveway of the residence. I had driven over the lawn and stopped right beside the bike in the driveway.

I started to get out of my cruiser, but before I could get off the seat, the driver got up, picked up the bike and off he went.

I turned to go out the driveway and realized the owner's mailbox was clearly in my way. I didn't have time to stop, back up and go around it. If I had, I surely would have lost too much ground on the motorcycle. So I ran over the mailbox. Yep, I ran right over it.

The post went down, but the mailbox broke loose, landing on the hood of my cruiser on the first bounce, the roof on the second bounce, the trunk on the third bounce and finally on the ground.

That must have looked nice to the bystanders.

We were sailing toward Dover-Foxcroft by skipping across Route 15. I had called the chase in over the radio and Cpl. Paul Davis was north of me, but I wasn't sure how close.

Fortunately for me, a left turn was coming up that would take us into the North Country and hopefully right at Cpl. Davis. We were approaching the Guilford Center Road, and sure enough, the biker made the left turn.

A couple of short miles along this road is a wicked sharp S-turn with a residence at the heart of the turn.

I was able to keep the bike in sight, but was not able to gain on it. My only hope was to push it toward Davis. I last saw the biker approaching the S-turn and he was leaning to the right, almost touching the pavement with his knee.

I, too, entered the S-turn at a high rate of speed and got the surprise of my life.

Right in the middle of the S-turn was an oncoming vehicle. Although there were no lines in the middle of the road, if there had been, he would have been sitting on the middle of it.

I saw his face which had wide eyes, and an even wider open mouth.

It was obvious he had just been scared a moment before by a motorcycle and was now being scared witless by a State Police cruiser.

Just beyond the motorist, who was taking up most of the road, was the residence I mentioned earlier. On the front lawn was the owner of that residence raking his front yard on this beautiful warm, sunny, peaceful spring day.

I had one maneuver available to me, which I took. I swerved hard to the right to miss the oncoming vehicle, then hard to the left to get back in the road and once again to the right to stay in the road.

I came to a sideways screeching halt, with smoke coming off my tires as I skidded to a stop.

While I was sliding to that stop, I watched as the lawn raker threw his rake in the air and hightailed it to the house.

I had missed the oncoming vehicle and the lawn raker had not really come close to being in danger, but I had an urge that I should at least say something to the startled man.

So I backed into his driveway and stopped beside him on the lawn.

Did you ever say something that you wished you could take back as soon as you said it? Well, this was one of those moments.

I rolled down my window and looked at the frightened man. He had the same expression that I had seen a few seconds before on the motorist.

"Pardon me, but did you see a motorcycle go through here?"

I kicked myself before I ever got the words completely out. I don't think I even waited for an answer, leaving the lawn raker dumbfounded as I drove away.

I went up around the corner, and there on the straightaway was Davis, out of his cruiser picking up his flashlight. I pulled up to Paul and he was just about as excited as I was.

He told me the bike was coming right at him. He got his flashlight and as the biker approached him, the hot rod exited the road and drove through the field and onto Butter Street, but not before a flashlight crashed into the spokes of the wheel. That was the last we saw of the bike that day.

I rushed back to the accident in Guilford, then Paul and I began investigating who was driving the bike. We were able to make a charge of failing to stop for a police officer on a local young man, but I lost the case in court months later for not being able to identify who the operator was on that wild, crazy ride through Guilford on that lovely spring day.

Just another day in the life.

Chop, Chop

To steal a line from my good friend, Warden John Ford, "Good often comes with the bad." And in the wonderful career of law enforcement, we had to find ways to deal and cope with human tragedy.

Some of the more serious situations we handled were, of course, domestic violence incidents. When I first joined the Maine State Police, the incidents were dealt with more leniently than they are now.

Here is one domestic incident from years ago that I handled. It was a beautiful spring day and I was trying to enjoy a day off at home cleaning up the lawn after a long winter at Moosehead Lake. It was late in the afternoon when a terrified acquaintance came racing into my driveway.

"Mark, Mark. You've got to help me," he yelled.

He was the husband of a woman who held a prominent position in town. She was always very nice to me, but, for sure, no one knows what goes on behind closed doors at home.

"What's wrong?" I asked. I had no idea what could be wrong with this mild-mannered person who was so well thought of in Greenville.

"My wife is drunk," he said. "And when she gets like that I just try to stay out of her way. But today she drank way too much. We were at home and she came up to me and took my glasses off my face and laid them on the counter. Then she got out the large meat cleaver and proceeded to chop my glasses into little pieces. All I could do was look at her while she was doing this. When she got done chopping them into little pieces, she looked at me and said, 'You're next!'"

"What did you do then," I asked, wide-eyed.

"I ran like hell," he said, still wound up like a top. "She chased me right out of the house. So I drove in town to find you."

"Thanks," I told him.

The man told me what his wife would be driving for a vehicle and that he was pretty sure she had chased him all the way to Greenville.

"I'm pretty sure she's downtown right now, Mark," he said. "This all happened about 10 minutes ago."

"All right," I said. "I've got to get on my uniform and I'll head right in and see if I can find her.

"Do you want her arrested for what she did to you?" I asked as I hurried away, not really waiting for an answer.

I went inside, threw on my uniform, jumped in the cruiser and headed toward town. Luck was on my side that day. As soon as I got into town, one of the first cars I met was the woman for whom I was looking. I let her drive by me, then flipped around and made a traffic stop. As I approached, she seemed very nonchalant about being stopped.

Once I was beside her driver's door and looked at her, there was no question in my mind that she was blitzed.

"What are you doing today, Dee?"

"I'm looking for that wimp of a husband of mine," she said. "I've got some unfinished business with him."

"Well, you've gone as far as you're going today," I said. "I'm arresting you for drunk driving."

"You can't do that!"

"Yes I can," I said and opened the door and escorted her out before she attempted to drive away. I have to say that she could drive better than she could walk that day. But she was all done and going with me. I never let her know that her husband had turned her in and kept the situation focused on the arrest for operating under the influence.

On the way to jail I had to ask. "So why are you looking for your husband?"

"Because he's a wimp and I am tired of being married to a wimp."

"Any other reason," I inquired.

"Nope."

And that was that. I took her to jail, where she was booked. While there, I called her husband, told him I had arrested his wife for OUI and asked him if he wanted to press charges with regard to his glasses. He did not.

Their marriage ended in divorce, and the ex-husband later told me that he slept much better after that.

Just another day in the life.

Hypothermia

Being a trooper requires dealing with a lot of tragedy. Perhaps the hardest part of the job, for me, was telling family members that a loved one had been killed and was never again coming home.

Sometimes one was a little easier than another to deliver the news, but it was always difficult and left a lasting impression on me.

This story is about one of those incidents. When I patrolled the northern area of Piscataquis County, I lived in the small town of Greenville Junction. My home was next door to the famous Dr. Pritham. Everyone in Greenville Junction knew each other and probably knew more than they should about everyone else's business. But it was a tight-knit group that helped each other when needed.

Late one middle-of-the-winter cold afternoon, a neighbor came to tell me that her brother was overdue from returning from a night of snowmobiling and camaraderie at a friend's camp.

She and the rest of her family were getting rather concerned that he had not made it home yet and it wasn't like her brother to not check in.

I gathered all the information I could from her so an investigation could be initiated. Once I got the location of the camp, I contacted Warden Charlie Davis, who patrolled the area. I advised him of the complaint, where the overdue person was last seen and where he was supposedly heading.

Warden Davis immediately went looking for the overdue person.

I re-interviewed my neighbor to find out who she had contacted when looking for her brother. I also asked for names of friends and relatives, in case he went somewhere different and never bothered to tell anyone. As soon as I finished talking with her and before I had made any calls, Warden Davis radioed that he had found the snowmobile. He gave me his location and I drove in to meet him there.

Warden Davis had searched the trail between the camp the man had left and the residence he was supposedly heading toward. The majority of the trail was on a plowed woods road. It was there that Warden Davis found a set of snowmobile tracks going up over a plowed snow bank.

We trudged up over the snow bank and found the snowmobile crashed into a tree. The sled was moderately damaged in the front end. There had been a dusting of snow overnight, but it didn't cover any of the evidence. We could easily see the operator was at the very least stunned and confused after striking the tree. We could see where he landed in the snow. There was a fair amount of blood, indicating he was injured.

Looking over the scene, we determined the operator had gotten up and wandered around the sled for a short period of time. The crash site was only about 10 feet from the plowed road, but the operator did not know this as it would have been very dark and the snow bank was high.

Instead of walking back up over the snow bank to the roadway to safety, the operator made a fatal mistake and wandered off in the opposite direction, deeper into the woods. I knew this meant serious trouble for the snowmobiler.

Warden Davis and I had only walked a couple of hundred yards into the woods when we came across an article of clothing. I knew immediately what that meant. The person was suffering from hypothermia.

I learned about hypothermia at the Maine State Police Academy. Hypothermia occurs when heat leaves a person's body and s/he eventually freezes to death.

One of the things I learned, and one that I had a hard time believing, was people suffering from hypothermia actually feel hot and want to take off their clothes. I could not believe anyone would do this in such a horrible, scary situation.

But here I was on my first such case and it seemed to be coming true right in front of my eyes. As we followed the trail deeper into the woods, Warden Davis and I came across another piece of clothing. Things looked dire.

After several hundred yards, we found the man. He was lying in the snow, his boots were off, and it appeared that he had been attempting to pull off his snowmobile suit when he died in the snow. He had frozen to death.

It was such a sad sight to see. The man had died in a state of confusion after being injured in the snowmobile accident and not being able to find his way out of trouble.

A simple, minor accident had taken his life.

Then it dawned on me that I had to tell my neighbor and this man's family what had happened to him. But first Warden Davis and I had to do a preliminary investigation to determine there was no foul play.

Afterward we put him on a toboggan to take him out of the woods so he could be transported to a funeral home.

When all of that was taken care of, I notified the family. Some people are able to figure out when a police officer arrives if the news is good or bad. When I arrived at the residence without their brother, they knew the news was tragic.

This was one lesson that I learned very early in my career; never take the elements for granted. Treat them like they could hurt you, because they can. Dress appropriately, even if going out for a short while.

Just another day in the life.

A Halloween Tradition in Unity

It's heartwarming when people create family traditions for the holidays. I know how much I look forward to our family Christmas Eve gathering. Along with a delicious turkey meal, we watch the young ones open Christmas presents and, best of all, spend time with the extended family and have a wonderful time.

This story is also about a tradition. It has nothing to do with a nice, warm gathering of people, though. Nope, it's about the annual dragging of an outhouse into the middle of the intersection of routes 9 and 139 in Unity—smack-dab in the middle of the town under the blinking traffic light.

It used to happen every Halloween. I was told of this wonderful tradition by none other than my Game Warden friend, John Ford, the first year I transferred into the area from the Moosehead Lake region.

"Oh, it's just some prank they play every year. We never seem to catch them, though, even though we usually learn much later from some camp owner of just where the outhouse came from," John said.

Sure enough, each and every Halloween, sooner or later, mostly later, an outhouse would appear in the middle of the intersection. It was actually quite funny. I always wanted to see it being dragged down the road by a pickup or whatever was used. But I never did.

One year, I thought it was time to put in some extra effort and see if I could catch the pranksters. It had been a quiet Halloween evening and when I made it to Unity, the outhouse had not yet made its grand appearance. It was late, so I thought I could do some surveillance and catch the tricksters. I found a spot to hide my cruiser and waited. And waited.

Did I tell you how I have no patience? I like to be moving.

Case in point: I thought one night I would repay John Boy and ride with him, as he used to almost live in my cruiser, but I had never ridden with him.

The night came for me to ride with John Boy. I jumped in and we went to Burnham to check fields. Then we chose one in which to sit. I loved riding around and checking things, but once we got into position in the back of the field, we were there about six minutes when I asked, "What do we do now?"

John started up his truck and drove me home.

So there I was this Halloween night sitting in the cruiser waiting for an outhouse to be dragged down the road. I watched vehicles passing by so I could see who was out in the middle of the night and who might be possible suspects. I think I made it about 90 minutes when I couldn't sit anymore. I had to do something.

Quietly, with my headlights off, I moved out of my position and made a quick pass through Unity College. It took all of five minutes, giving me a nice break from sitting still and seeing something different than an intersection. Once I cruised through the campus, I headed back to my downtown hiding spot.

Apparently, the pranksters had more patience than I did and my hiding spot wasn't as good as I thought it was. Because right there in the middle of the intersection was an outhouse. A nice one, too. I couldn't believe it.

Obviously, the outhouse bandits had been watching me and waiting for the opportunity to drag it there, then make a hasty retreat.

The problem with that particular area for law enforcement officers was, there were seven different routes of escape. I knew I had not passed any vehicles, so I chose another route. I couldn't be that far behind the trick-or-treaters, as it had been done just minutes before.

No such luck. I chose the wrong avenue and never saw a thing. I turned to go back to the intersection to call a wrecker to have the outhouse removed. I was shaking my head that the Halloween pranksters had, once again, tricked me.

As I was approaching the outhouse, I saw a pickup truck travel down Main Street approaching the intersection. It promptly smacked right into the outhouse, leaving nothing but a lot of kindling wood all over the road.

It literally exploded.

The only whole thing left was the toilet seat in the middle of the road. I couldn't help but laugh at the situation and wondered if the driver of the pickup knew what he ran into.

I stopped the motorist and approached him. There was kindling wood all over his truck.

Yep, he was drunk. And was wondering what in the world he had just hit. I don't think he believed me when I told him he ran over an outhouse.

Just another quiet evening in Waldo County.

You're Going to be Okay

"You never know what is going to happen from one moment to the next."

It's a phrase we hear and speak throughout our career being troopers. It's mind-boggling in this profession how we can go from being in a boring routine to sheer terror in seconds.

We did things in this career we never thought possible. Scary, life-altering incidents happened, and more often than most ever realize, even here in the good old safe state of Maine.

This particular story is just that—scary. I was working in the China area, tying up loose ends on several cases. It was a Sunday evening, usually a night when most people were winding down from an active weekend and getting ready for work the following day.

I worked some criminal investigations, catching people at home, did some interviews and gathered information I needed to proceed further with cases.

It was kind of a ho-hum, one-foot-in-front-of-the-other kind of thing.

Then a call of a domestic situation came in to Maine State Police headquarters. The call was for a trooper in Troop C, but he was quite a distance away. I was a lot closer and could be there in fewer than 10 minutes, so I headed to the residence until the responding trooper could arrive. It was a good thing I did. Before I got there, the situation turned very violent and a child witnessed the horror.

I pulled into the trailer park and a young boy was standing at the end of his driveway in tears. He ran to my cruiser and sobbed, "My daddy's been stabbed! He's lying on the kitchen floor!"

It is hard to ever forget the look on such a young, innocent child's face. It was one of sheer terror. He had no idea what was going to happen. All I could do was my very best at making it better for him and keeping him safe. I told him to point me to the right location so I could help his dad. He also told me his mom was inside and she was the one who stabbed him.

I told the little boy, "Stand right by my cruiser and don't move. There will be another trooper arriving here shortly and you tell him right where I am. Can you do that for me?"

"Yes," he said.

I entered the trailer and the man was lying on his back on the kitchen floor. He had a knife sticking out of his chest. He was ashen white and tried to talk with me. While kneeling beside him, comforting him, and listening to him, I was very concerned about the location of his attacker.

Could she be lurking behind a corner waiting to attack again? I had to console the victim and keep a watchful eye out for the attacker.

You never know how people will react when police get involved. I had been at a domestic situation before when a man had beaten his wife and when I went to arrest the man, the woman physically attacked me, begging me not to take her man to jail. I had to fight off the female as well. We had to be prepared for about anything.

Kneeling beside the victim, I called for medical assistance by portable radio to Maine State Police HQ. While talking on the radio, I finally located the little boy's mom.

She was in the darkened living room, sitting in an overstuffed chair staring into space. She didn't seem to be a threat at that moment and once I had help coming for the man and he was comfortable, albeit with a knife sticking out of his chest, I made my way to the living room to confront the female.

When I stood in front of her she was barely aware that I was there. There were empty prescription bottles beside her and she nodded yes to me after inquiring if she had swallowed all of the pills that the bottles had contained. She was barely coherent and also needed immediate medical assistance. I again radioed SP Augusta for another ambulance to get them both to the hospital.

The other trooper arrived on scene, followed closely by ambulances. Both people were triaged and loaded into the ambulances. We didn't know until much later how they made out.

At that moment, the most important thing was to take care of the little boy. As the other trooper talked with the boy, the trooper learned he knew many of the little boy's friends, family and relatives. The little boy desperately wanted to stay with one of his relatives, so he was whisked away to that location. We assured him he had done nothing wrong and that hopefully everything would be OK.

Both the man and woman survived the ordeal. Charges were brought against her and she was dealt with in the court system. This incident occurred shortly before my retirement, and I never learned what became of the family. I often think of that little boy and how sad it was for him to go through such an ordeal at his age. It's hard to fathom how in the world things could get so bad to resort to that type of violence.

"You never know what is going to happen from one moment to the next!"

Just another day in the life.

Lockdown

This story reminds me of how much things have changed since the 1980s in state government. When I joined the Maine State Police in 1977, troopers worked six days a week and were on duty 24 hours a day.

We had to put in a minimum of 10 hours per day "on the road." All the other duties, including cleaning cruisers, polishing gear and doing paperwork, had to be done outside of that 10 hours.

We either had to be on the radio or at a phone number where we could be immediately reached. There were no pagers, portable radios, cell phones or computers. There was no overtime pay when we got called out or worked beyond the 10-hour minimum. We also were not paid when we were in court on our day off. Three hundred-plus work hours per month was the norm back then.

My time slips from that period indicated that many times I left for work on a Friday night and returned home for the first time Sunday afternoon, when things finally slowed down. Forty-plus straight hours of work was common during the first eight years of my career with the Maine State Police.

But, I have to admit, it was the best time to be a trooper. I was young, full of energy and couldn't get enough of being a trooper. I knew almost everyone in my patrol area and if something bad happened, I was usually right in the middle of it.

This particular story, though, shows how much control the state had over us. It was 1980 and the Maine State Prison guards and administration no longer had control of the State Prison in Thomaston. Inmates called the shots and some lived better than people on the outside.

One of the principal players was a prisoner nicknamed Fat Jack. It seemed as though everything had to be run by him before it could be done. His cell was furnished better than most homes, with an overstuffed recliner as his throne.

The state intended to regain control of the prison, which meant the Maine State Police had to go inside and, along with the prison guards, lock down the prison and clean it out.

I remember getting my marching orders. I was ordered to head to the Maine State Police Academy in Waterville, where close to 100 troopers would muster and get assignments.

The first wave of troopers had already entered the prison and locked it down. The reports we got at the Academy were not pleasant.

Those who gave troopers a difficult time were dealt with harshly. I'm not referring to prisoners being uncooperative or mouthy; for the most part, that is part of the job of being a police officer.

What some prisoners were doing were using metal pails as toilets, saving it up and when troopers arrived to take control, the prisoners threw pails of human waste at the troopers. To be honest, I didn't like what I heard.

After getting our assignments, we left our cruisers at the Academy, boarded the "Gray Ghost," (our nickname for a converted school bus that transported us around during our days at the Academy) and rode to Thomaston to enter the Maine State Prison.

I have to tell you, I lucked out. I was assigned to an outside wall in a watchtower. I was armed with a high-powered rifle and had orders to shoot anyone who attempted to climb the wall and escape.

But there were no prisoners outside; they were all locked up inside. So I stared at an empty yard for 12 hours, bored out of my mind.

What did I get for a break? Prison food and a nap on the floor of the command center inside the prison. This routine went on for days. It was clearly one of my worst assignments during my entire career with the Maine State Police.

Once the prison was cleared, searched, and secured, we were free to head home. But, of course, first came the ride back to Waterville on the Gray Ghost.

Once there, I got in my cruiser and boogied as quickly as I could back to the wonderful little town of Greenville Junction.

I remember arriving at home and pulling into the driveway. I was so tired, after not having any good sleep for almost a week that I didn't even put my cruiser inside the garage. (A move that I soon regretted.) I crawled inside, made my way to the couch and collapsed, sleeping for hours.

But the life of a trooper never really slows down. I was jolted awake but did not know why. It was after midnight and I decided that I should go out on patrol as I had not been around for days.

I wandered out to my cruiser and reached for the door handle. Why in the world was the door handle so low to the ground was my immediate thought. I had to bend way down to reach my door handle.

I stepped back and took a look. My cruiser was almost sitting on its frame in the driveway. All four tires were flat as pancakes. I dug out my flashlight and looked at the tires. All four had been slashed. I guess I had discovered what had jolted me awake.

Then it dawned on me why this had been done.

Remembering the big case I had recently investigated that consumed years of my career, today was arraignment day for the big fish who got netted in that case.

And the bar he hung out at was within sight of my home. At that moment, though, I was too tired to care. There would be another day to catch that guy. I simply went back inside and went to bed,

Just another day in the life.

The Puking Drunk

One evening I had to attend a section meeting in Corinna. Coming out of the North Woods of Moosehead Lake, I hooked up with Cpl. Paul Davis so we could ride together.

We connected in the Sangerville area, and Paul jumped in with me for the ride. Mandatory section meetings were held about once a month. They were more like training sessions, as we got updates on laws, policies, goings-on and whatever else needed to be discussed.

They were a pain in the butt to attend, but it was a time to visit with other guys in the section who you normally didn't get a chance to see very often.

Paul and I had just gone through Dexter and were heading south on Route 7 when we came across a vehicle parked at a very strange angle on the side of the road half in and half out of the driving lane. It quickly caught our attention.

As we got closer, we could see why the vehicle was parked at such an angle. The driver's door was open and the driver had simply leaned out the door and was puking his guts out into the southbound lane of Route 7.

Paul and I stopped to render assistance to the sickly man. As we approached the driver, he painfully lifted his head to look at us. It didn't take a rocket scientist to realize this guy wasn't just sick, he was beyond drunk.

The only thing coming out of his mouth was booze that could no longer fit into his stomach. He had a passenger in the front seat who was passed out and drunk to boot. When the man was finally able to speak to us, which took a while, and when we could figure out what he was saying, we realized he was quite the comedian.

Can you believe he was not happy to see us?

Fortunately for him, the law at that time did not allow us to arrest him for drunk driving even though we could prove operation.

So we made arrangements for the two men and took them to a residence down a side road about a mile off Route 7 going toward Ripley. Paul drove them, and I followed along behind.

After getting them to the farmhouse and giving them a stern warning about not driving until they sobered up, Paul and I headed off to the meeting in Corinna. For them to sober up would take days.

The meeting went by fairly quickly and Paul and I headed north for a night of work. As we were coming out of Corinna, I mentioned to Paul that we should check on our two buddies to see if they had stayed put.

So we headed to the farm where we left them. We slowly drove down the road until the farmhouse was in sight. Lo and behold the vehicle was still there. We thought it was pretty good that they had decided to stay off the road.

But just then, as if they had been waiting for us, we saw activity in the driveway and the same two guys got into the vehicle and drove away from the farmhouse heading in the opposite direction from us. We could not believe what we were seeing.

When I say they were beyond drunk, I mean when we left them, these guys were barely coherent. A vehicle was no place for them. We watched them leave the driveway, turn onto the road and head toward Ripley.

With two people in a vehicle, a lot of times we drove alongside the suspect vehicle and shined a light into it so we could positively identify the operator.

Thank goodness we did it this time. I pulled alongside the suspect vehicle, and Paul shined his flashlight on the operator. Though it was not funny, we could do nothing but laugh. The operator was so drunk he was using the steering wheel to hold up his head.

His head was literally resting on the wheel and he was looking through the wheel to see out the windshield. Ever so slowly, he looked to his left and looked right at us. We definitely could ID him after the stop. And this time, the law had been clearly violated and we could arrest him for the OUI offense.

I turned on the blue lights and he stopped right in the roadway. I stopped behind him, and Paul and I approached the operator.

It got even better.

When I opened the door, the driver was sitting in the middle of the seat with his buddy. With his head hanging and his eyes barely open, he pointed out of the vehicle and drawled, "The driver just ran out across that field!"

If I had not just witnessed all this, his lie would have been possible to believe, as no one could fathom how this guy could have driven a vehicle in his condition. But I knew what I had just seen, and this drunk had just won a place in my front seat.

Paul and I removed him from the vehicle and brought him back to my cruiser to process him for OUI. He protested all the way, denied he ever drove and though he did as he was told, he never admitted to driving the vehicle. It was still a great case with lots of evidence and this was definitely headed to court.

However, the entertainment was just beginning. After processing the operator for OUI, we bailed him on personal recognizance and took him and his friend back to their home in Ripley. One guy had to stay awake to give directions, and we finally arrived at the homestead.

They lived quite a ways into the woods all by themselves on a narrow dirt road in a little mobile home that sat on a small knoll. The trailer was surrounded by trees. The driveway stopped right in front of the knoll, and people had to navigate the small knoll to get to the entrance of the trailer.

The first thing we did was awaken our drunks. They seemed to have gone to sleep in the back of my cruiser within minutes. After getting them awake and out of my cruiser, I announced they were home and free to go inside. They had a court date, and I would see the operator then. Paul and I got back into my cruiser, and we waited for them to get inside before we left.

What happened next was one of the funniest things I witnessed in my career, though very sad at the same time.

The two drunk buddies had to walk about 20 feet to the rise, up the three-foot knoll and take two steps up into the trailer and they would be home free.

Well, they made it to the knoll but as each tried to climb it, he fell over and rolled down to the driveway in front of my cruiser.

After each had fallen a half-dozen times, they decided to lock arms and navigate the knoll together. They still never made it to the top. The two drunks simply fell over and rolled down the hill together rolling over each other. It reminded me of Red Skelton doing the "Freddie the Freeloader" skit on TV.

Paul and I laughed until it hurt and tears streamed down our cheeks. After they had their fun, Paul and I assisted them into the trailer. Before we departed, we warned them not to leave, as they might not ever get back into the trailer.

A sad footnote to this story is the driver, who was only in his 40s, passed away before the court date for his OUI.

Just another quiet evening.

Dennis and Skipper

The following story, which will be in two parts, is a conversation I had with Retired Maine State Police Lt. Dennis Hayden. Dennis was the first certified K9 handler with the first certified K9, Skipper. The conversation, as always whenever I talk with Dennis, is heavily edited.

The following is a history of how the K9 program got started in the Maine State Police. So sit back and enjoy a little history of our department.

It was 1980 and the department was lead back then by Col. Allan Weeks. His administration decided to start a K9 program after being approached by Sgt. Lloyd Williams and Trooper Denny McLellan from Troop E, which covers the Penobscot, Hancock and Washington areas. Both had dogs that they had trained on their own, and they were having quite a bit of success.

It was arranged through the Connecticut State Police, which had a K9 program since the early 1960s, that whomever was chosen for training would be trained and housed in Connecticut at no cost.

Col. Weeks decided to send two troopers the first time. Sgt. Williams issued a memo to any and all troopers interested in being a K9 handler to apply. So then-Trooper Dennis Hayden did just that. After the application process, which included an oral board, two troopers were selected — Dennis was first and Trooper William "Bill" Bruso was second.

Sgt. Williams took the results to the colonel. Reportedly, Col. Weeks said something to the effect, "There's no way in hell I'm sending those two together out of state for any reason!"

To put it mildly, both Dennis and Bill were like bulls in China closets and heaven forbid anything or anyone get in their way. So Col. Weeks decided one would go first. Since Dennis was first on the list, he got to go to Connecticut.

And this is how Skipper came to the K9 program. Skipper, who was from a kennel in Skowhegan, had a long name that came with his certificate.

The woman who ran the kennel, Mrs. Rath, sold Skipper to an older couple. They took him home and tied him to a tree in the yard. He was about 14 months old at the time, and one day when the woman went to feed Skipper, he growled at her. The lady got quite scared and called Mrs. Rath to come get him.

Mrs. Rath called Deputy Tom Seger, who worked for the Piscataquis County Sheriff's Office, because he had a dog and she had dealt with him before. Unable to stand the thought of putting down such a handsome, big dog, Mrs. Rath offered Skipper to Tom and told Tom to come get him.

Tom learned the Maine State Police was starting a K9 program and offered the dog to the Maine State Police. So Dennis drove to Dover-Foxcroft, picked up Skipper, and brought him home to Vassalboro.

"My wife thought I was going to go and pick up this cute, cuddly, little puppy and I brought home this 100-pound dog," said Dennis. "I drove into the yard, let Skipper out of the cruiser, brought him into the house and the first thing he did was run into our bedroom and take a big smelly dump on the floor. It was a great start with Skipper and my wife."

I sometimes wonder if Mrs. Rath had the foresight to know Skipper was a special dog that was going to do great things in his future.

When Dennis finished the 12-week school in Connecticut, he and Skipper were the first certified K9 team for the Maine State Police. Bill Bruso, who was the second certified K9 handler for the Maine State Police, was actually sent to Massachusetts State Police, which was starting a new canine program.

After their training, a K9 unit was put in place for the department; led by Sgt. Lloyd Williams with Dennis of Troop C, Bruso of Troop B, and Denny McLellan of Troop E. Canine activities were in addition to regular working hours for the troopers. The men and dogs put in a lot of hours.

Even though Denny and his dog, Ben, were not a certified K9 team, they worked the northern part of the state. Ben was a good dog. Sgt. Williams' dog was more of a show dog, and he did not do much road work.

Bill and Dennis did the majority of work. Dennis was on the road all the time with Skipper, going all over the state. Of course, Skipper was a really good dog, and as he got to be better known by local police agencies and other agencies, Dennis got called constantly for Skipper's services.

Most of the calls were for tracking—suspects of burglaries, car thefts and fleeing night hunters.

Sentinel Photo by Dick Maxwell

Trooper's Best Friend

Trooper Dennis Hayden of Vassalboro accepts congratulations for
both himself and his specially trained police dog, Skipper, from
Col. Allan H. Weeks, chief of the Maine State Police. State Police
Troop C of Skowhegan turned out in force for its annual inspection
by Col. Weeks and Commissioner of Public Safety Arthur A.
Stilphen (upper left) Friday at the Waterville Armory. Story on
Page 3.

*L-R Commissioner Stilphen, Tr. Dave Viles, Colonel Allan Weeks,
Tr. Mark Nickerson, Tr. Dennis Hayden and his K9, Skipper.*

"All kinds of things like that and Skipper was very successful at it. The dog was just good. It didn't matter if we were in the city or in the country, Skipper could do it all. He was nuts, but he was good," said Hayden.

A lot of people used to compare Dennis with his dog.

"Skipper was crazy in the car. Whenever I would key the mic to talk with SP Augusta, the dog would get right in my ear and bark nonstop. He would get all wound up," said Hayden.

"One time, I got in a pretty serious cruiser accident in Winthrop. The cruiser rolled over and slid a long ways upside down, crashing into a tree. When the cruiser finally came to a stop, I was worried about Skipper as I could not find him," said Hayden.

"When I looked outside, there he was, standing on all fours and peering inside the cruiser to see if I was all right. After that crash, every time I would accelerate hard, the dog would go berserk and bite me. It was almost like he was saying to me, 'OK Dad, we're not going upside down again are we?'

"If I started to follow a suspected drunk driver and was observing poor operation of the vehicle, I would rest my hand on the blue light switch, waiting for the right moment to turn them on. Skipper had that all figured out," Dennis said. "He would start to get excited, then he would pace back and forth and it was like him telling me, 'OK, OK, we've seen enough. He's over the line, let's go, let's go!'"

"If I patrolled during the day, Skipper would stay right in the car. But at nighttime, if I was up to a violator's car, he would jump out of the cruiser, come up and walk around the violator's car, walk around me, kind of bumping me when he walked by and go back into the cruiser. I never taught him that," said Dennis. "And he would only do it at nighttime. I had had a few fights with some violators and apparently he just wanted the bad guys to know he was around.

"Sometimes I would be talking with a violator and when Skipper walked through the headlights, it would startle them and they would go, 'What's that?' I would just tell them, 'Oh, don't worry, that's just my dog.' I am sure he defused many situations.

"Skipper really liked to work—he just loved it. If the phone rang in the middle of the night, he would be right beside the bed, waiting for me to get up. If I only talked on the phone, and didn't have to leave home, you could tell he was [ticked] off that he was not going to work. If I ever left him home when I went to work [like going to court], he would get so [upset]. He would sulk and not even come around me. He'd act like a great big spoiled kid. If I went near him, he would growl and grumble. He was a very vocal animal, anyway," said Hayden.

When I was a trooper in Greenville, Dennis did a K9 presentation for the local Boy Scout troop. This was my first real interaction with Skipper, except for a few run-ins at the Skowhegan barrack. I think I was as impressed with his demonstration as any of the Scouts.

His dog was smart, friendly when he wanted to be, and vicious when told to be. Dennis used me as a prop when he put Skipper through some of his paces. Skipper would allow the boys to literally maul him, then Dennis told

Skipper to watch me. I didn't dare move as I stood there being "watched" by this monster of a dog.

I have no idea what the next command was, but with Dennis holding a leash around his neck, Skipper's next move scared the crap out of me. He growled, showed his teeth, and pulled hard on his leash. I stood there not daring to even breath.

With another command from Dennis, Skipper was again my friend and came over wanting to be petted.

Of course, getting into Dennis' cruiser with Skipper in the back was a whole new experience in how to get into a car. Once I opened the door and reached in, Skipper had my arm in his mouth. I didn't dare move until Dennis called off the dog. When I rode with Dennis, Skipper placed his head right beside my head. Believe me, I never made any sudden moves in that cruiser.

Stay tuned for Part II, where I will tell you about some of the many major accomplishments and exploits of this brave dog.

Dennis and Skipper - Part II

In Part I, I explained how the Maine State Police K9 program began and wrote about its first certified K9 team. I also described some of the traits of both the handler, retired Lt. Dennis Hayden and his dog, Skipper.

In this part, I am going to describe some of the major cases that this K9 team worked on and solved.

Part II of this column also comes from an interview with Dennis, which, again, is heavily edited.

One of Skipper's traits I did not talk about last time was his absolute dedication and loyalty to his handler. Both members of this team were clearly one. The following tidbit proves this beyond any doubt.

"I was going through Winslow one night, and it was cold as hell," said Hayden. "I had made a traffic stop and didn't roll my window down, which we are trained to do so the dog can get out if I needed any help. So this one night, I got this guy out, and was going through the OUI process and made the arrest. I was bringing him back to the cruiser, not handcuffed because I rarely did that and Skipper went nuts, anyway, because he hated handcuffs. And just as I was reaching for the door handle, I could tell this guy was going to make a run for it, and sure enough, off he goes.

"So I take off running down the street after him. It wasn't long before I'm thinking, 'OK, where's my dog? If he doesn't hurry up and get here, I am going to kick his [butt] when I get back to the cruiser.'

"So I had to pick it up and run a little faster to catch this guy. I tackled him, rolled around, handcuffed him, and huffed and puffed. As I am walking back to my cruiser with this guy I am getting more mad at my dog than anything because he never came to help me.

"I get to my cruiser, opened the door and Skipper had eaten the inside of my cruiser. He couldn't get out. I forgot to roll the window down. He had eaten my steering wheel, tore the headliner down, ripped up the seats—he even scratched the windshield trying to get out to help me.

"I had the hardest time getting my suspect into the cruiser, Skipper was literally trying to eat him. When I got him to jail, his jacket was almost torn off from him. It was shredded by the dog. And I only had to go over the bridge into Waterville to the police station.

When we got there, the suspect asked me, 'What happened to my jacket?' I told him, 'Don't you remember? We got into a fight and it got ripped. You know, we rolled around on the ground and things happen.'

"When I got back in the cruiser, the back seat was full of little pieces of this guy's jacket. I have to take the blame for this one, it was my fault for not rolling down the window."

"One evening I had gassed up my cruiser at HQ in Augusta and afterwards was coming down Stone Street in Augusta. Officer Paul Reitchel of the Augusta Police Department had a car stopped and he was in a hell of a fight with two guys in the street.

"One guy was even kicking at him. I bailed out and went running down the street after one of the guys. Skipper ran past me like a rocket and absolutely just nailed the guy that Paul was fighting with. Skipper just latched onto him. "Paul goes, 'Hi, Skip!' Skipper was chewing the hell out of this guy, he knew the difference between a uniform and a bad guy. He was just a great dog, he put an end to that fight so quick.

"One of the governors came out and said he did not want any crowd control done with the dogs. But I could put him on a leash and put him out in front of me. Skipper would just spin back and forth. I could walk through any crowd and no one could get to me. No one could even touch me. That dog could be one of the most vicious creatures I ever saw. They used to call him 'the alligator with fur.' Skipper loved kids, but when it was time to work, it was time to work.

"One time I had been approached by a guy that had lost his eyeglasses. They were special glasses and very expensive. It would also be quite a while before he could get them replaced. He had lost them in a field a few days earlier and could not find them. I didn't think we could find them either, but I was willing to give it a try. The guy took me to where he thought he lost them and I put Skipper to work ... Skipper found them in about two hours.

"We had a lost child over in Farmington one night. The boy was only 6 years old. It had been hours since the call came in. The scene had been so contaminated. So many people had gone every which way. Skipper had to work through the whole mess and once he made it to the woods, that was it. It took Skipper only one hour and he had that little boy. All [was] safe and sound when we brought him out of the woods.

"[I] got another call one night for a lost guy in Norridgewock. He had gone out in the woods and had been lost for two days. And they had bazillions of people looking all over for him. And within two hours of getting there, Skipper had found him and we brought him out of the woods. Skipper could just track. Get him in the woods and get him going, there wasn't much he would miss.

"Skipper was also good at obtaining statements from people. I would explain...that I [might] not know if [they] were lying or not but animals have that sixth sense and they can sense when someone is not telling the truth. And people would agree with me. So after asking questions, I would ask Skipper if the guy was lying, and the dog would growl. So I would warn my suspect that [they] better not be lying. 'My dog gets upset when people lie and when he gets upset, I can't hold him back.'

"We had this one guy from...the Midcoast. He was clearly one of the biggest well-known criminals in that area. This guy had again...escaped from prison and was running around telling everyone that he wasn't going to be taken alive this time. We worked this case for a while and finally learned that he was hiding out in the Greene area.

"So Skipper and I get in the area and work our way down and there he was, lying with his girlfriend under a blanket. We ended up jumping him. We had guns out and everything and I told him not to move. We pulled the blanket off from them and pulled the girl out of the way. And he was lying there with his hands underneath his body. We kept yelling at him to put his hands out, he wouldn't do it, so finally we warned him that the dog was next.

"He still would not comply, and he started to roll and when he did that, Skipper reached and grabbed him right by the cheek of his rear end. And Skipper picked him right up. This guy was no little guy, he went about 200 pounds. So Skipper had picked him up and absolutely just started chewing on him. I pulled Skipper off and we got the bad guy handcuffed. He had four huge bite marks on the cheeks of his butt.

"We were sued—me, the dog [and] the state. In federal court, [the prisoner] claimed that he was so traumatized, that he could not do anything of value with his life anymore. The guy was a [multiple-time] convicted felon, but he was claiming he was destroyed by this dog. He could not be a postman because of his newfound fear of dogs and being bitten by Skipper. This guy was pleading that he didn't do anything wrong and the judge just kind of said, 'Yeah right. See you later.'

"This is one of those cases where Col. Weeks called me up and asked, 'Dennis, is this a good bite? Because we are getting sued and the insurance companies want to settle with this guy.'

"And I asked the colonel, 'Do you want to give any money to this guy?' And the colonel said, 'Absolutely not. But I want to check with you and make sure this is a good bite.'

"I told him, 'Yes sir, this is by the book.' Col. Weeks said, 'Good enough for me. I'll sign off on it and let it go to court.'

"The lawyers fought it and it went to federal court. We won. Not one penny should have gone to this criminal, and it didn't.

"This next incident—the Moody Mountain manhunt—is about two convicts who escaped from the Maine State Prison in Thomaston and had been on the run for about two weeks. They had worked their way up the coast and were finally spotted on Moody Mountain in Searsmont.

"One of the convicts had shot Denny McLellan's dog, Ben.

"Skipper had been on that track for over four hours that day. It was terribly hot and humid, but Skipper would not give up. But I could see him wobbling (heat exhaustion), so I pulled him off. I had Denny come down with his dog, Ben, and gave them a starting point where we were hot on their trail. I took Skipper and got him into a stream to cool him down. Denny and his dog, along with Warden John Ford, had not gone 500 feet when they encountered those guys and they shot Denny's dog. So we almost had them before Skipper was just about to drop. Denny's dog did survive the shooting, but he was never the same after that. We lost the escapees after that once again.

"It wasn't too long afterwards when we got another call that these guys had broken into a home in the Searsmont area. The owners had come home and surprised them. They were cooking a meal when the owners came into the house. Once again, these guys were on the run. I got the call and got in the area. I remember Capt. LaMontagne saying it was a waste of time; we should get the bloodhounds down here so we can get these guys. I told him, 'Let me try,

Captain.' He mumbled back, 'We have been down here for two weeks and still have not gotten these guys.'

"I harnessed up and within 40 minutes, Warden John Ford and I had them both. [It was the] largest manhunt in the state of Maine. It was pouring rain that day, too. We got down in there, just before dark. I could see up ahead and they had put up a plastic tarp in the trees.

"I told John, 'They're right in front of us, right now.' We jumped on them before they could reach their gun. Skipper was right in their face. It was as if he knew it was the guys that had shot the other dog. I had kept Skipper back just enough so he couldn't get a piece of them, but they knew we meant business that day. We got them handcuffed and brought them back out of the woods. I asked the captain if he still needed the bloodhounds. 'No, I guess not,' he said. The captain actually took me out to Hazel Green's restaurant in Augusta and treated me to a steak dinner after he saw what the dog could do.

"I got called down to Northport one night. This guy had already shot one guy in the stomach and taken a second guy hostage. Once he heard the cruisers and the sirens, he left his hostage and took off into the woods.

"He was armed and saying he might as well kill a few pigs (police) before he died. Believe it or not, but Skipper was not that aggressive when he found what he was tracking. It was due to my tracking children and other stuff. He would just go up and put his nose on your cheek. I had to keep a leash on him so he wouldn't get too far ahead of me.

"Sgt. David Lindahl of the Maine State Police was with me on this track. I could tell we were close, because Skipper was pulling real hard on his harness. Then I fell into a hole and Skipper got away from me. When we caught up to Skipper again, he was standing right next to the guy, who was hiding beside a tree in the woods.

"But it was dark and the guy never saw Skipper. I thought he was going to shoot my dog, because Skipper was just standing there beside him. I kept calling Skipper back and he finally came. There were lots of exchanges between us and I lit up [the suspect] with the flashlight. He had the rifle right on us and was threatening to kill us. I told Dave right where he was. 'When I light him up again, you shoot him,' I said.

"I turned my light on the guy once again and when I did, the guy shot himself in the head. Dave also fired when I lit him up, hitting him in the butt. The guy was already dead, though, from his own hand. While we were waiting for the Attorney General's Office to [arrive], Skipper went over and relieved himself on the dead guy. I had to explain to them when they got there the yellow stain was from my dog."

There comes a time when a dog gets to retire and become the family pet. This was no exception in the Hayden family. Skipper had done his job and done it well and deserved his last few years to take it easy. But it was not to be for this dog with such a huge reputation. Even in retirement, Dennis got calls to track with Skipper, even though Dennis had transferred to the drug unit.

The following incident happened in Augusta, after Skipper was retired.

"I got a call one night that the Augusta Police Department had this missing 15-year-old girl. She had gone for a walk in the arboretum across from the Augusta Mental Health Institution. They couldn't find her and had everyone there looking for her this evening. They wanted to know if I could bring Skipper in.

"I still had my harness and stuff, but I told them [that I didn't] even have a cruiser to get him there with. I used my wife's little station wagon, threw Skipper in the back, got my harness and headed into Augusta. The Augusta officers showed me where she had last been seen. [Officers and K9s] had been looking for her for hours; it took Skipper just about 45 minutes when we found her. She had been stabbed to death by [a] patient from AMHI."

Skipper had once again done his job, even in retirement.

"Skipper retired officially in 1987. I had him another five years after he retired. He was almost 14 when he died."

This last part is not from an interview with Dennis, but what I remember when I heard that Skipper had been put down.

Upon hearing the news about Skipper, I ran into Dennis one day and offered my condolences. Dennis told me Skipper was suffering, he could barely walk anymore.

"I knew it was time. I made the appointment and took him in to the vet," said Hayden. "The vet put a shot in him and said it [would] not be long now. In a little bit the vet came back to the room. Skipper was lying on the floor...with his head in my lap, but he was still breathing.

"The vet said, 'I have never seen an animal take two shots to go.' And I told him, 'This is not your usual dog, Doc.'

"The vet gave him one more shot and Skipper slipped away. I laid down with him and bawled my eyes out while he died. It was the hardest thing I ever did. He was one hell of a dog."

And that is the story of the first certified Maine State Police K9 team and some of its exploits while serving the citizens of the state of Maine.

Home Improvement

One of my favorite TV shows is the sitcom *Home Improvement*. I love the dry humor and the advice that Wilson, the neighbor at the fence, dispenses to Tim.

Recently I watched the episode in which Tim's son got a used car and it ended up getting stolen and stripped of parts that were sold through a "chop shop."

Of course, Al had dripped boysenberry jam on the engine manifold when the son bought the car and that's eventually how the part was identified from the chop shop.

I had a similar case.

It started with my criminal friend, "Eddie." He had a really nice '68 Firebird that he was slowly restoring after an accident. Parts for this vehicle were sometimes hard to come by and could be quite expensive.

I watched from afar as he slowly brought this car back together. I love older cars, particularly muscle cars from the 60s—and this vehicle perfectly fit the bill. So it was fun to watch, even though it was from afar. Eddie wasn't someone I hung around with, I just kept arresting him throughout the years.

Then, one day, all of a sudden, bam, the car was finished. It did not seem right as it took Eddie quite a bit of time to get to various points of completion and then the car sat for months.

Now, the car was finished and it looked really good. I took notice of the change in the hood—the refinished car had a different hood with factory air scoops.

My sixth sense kicked in and I thought something was up. How was Eddie able to finish the vehicle and get those parts in such a short period of time?

One day not long after making these observations, I got a phone call from a trooper in another part of the state. "Hey Mark, do you know an Eddie who lives in the Unity area?"

"Why yes I do. Why do you ask?" I asked.

"Well, I've had this Pontiac Firebird stolen from this couple. The guy had spent years, and about $20,000, restoring it. He had the extra parts for sale and this Eddie came and looked at the stuff a couple of times. I don't have any evidence that he stole the car but I am curious as he came here a couple of times and then the car ended up stolen," the trooper said.

"Eddie has a Firebird of his own and he just finished up a restoration on his vehicle," I told the trooper. "Can you send me your report and do you mind if I contact your complainant?"

"Not at all, I'll send the report to you with all the numbers and information," he said.

Knowing Eddie, I knew he would not talk with me unless I had proof. I received the criminal report from the trooper and poured over the information.

I checked the VIN number from the stolen car against Eddie's. Of course I did this when he wasn't around. The numbers did not match—which meant Eddie kept the core part of his car and added to it. I looked the car over really good and took notes about what parts were on it and if there was anything unique about it. It was pretty much restored to the original specs.

After getting frustrated, I contacted the owners of the stolen Firebird. After they told me their story, I was certain that Eddie had stolen their vehicle.

The problem was, where is it now? I asked them if there was any part that might be unique and able to be identified.

That's when he told me that he had drilled a hole in the hood that was in the wrong place. He had to fix the outer part of the hood, but the hole still existed on the underside, because, as he said, it wouldn't show. The hole was to put the emblem on the hood.

I knew of another Firebird in the area and spoke to the owner. I asked him if he would let me look at the underside of his hood so I could see where the holes were for mounting the emblems. He was cooperative as I got under the hood and checked out the area and learned where the holes needed to be.

"Why in the world do you need to see that?" he asked.

"Oh, just curious," I said as I continued to take measurements and photos of the holes.

Even though I didn't have much, I didn't think I was going to get much more so it was time to approach Eddie and talk with him about his Firebird.

I made the approach in a friendly sort of way, showing more interest in the car and how nice it came out rather than being a trooper trying to pressure Eddie and asking too many questions.

We got talking about what he did to the motor and I asked if I could see it. Eddie opened the hood and I had a chance to check out the hood and see if it was the stolen one. Sure enough, there was the hole described to me by the victim of the stolen Firebird.

I acted like nothing was wrong and kept talking with Eddie about his restoration. He was enthusiastic as he described how he did the whole project.

I backed off, deciding to gather a little more evidence before making an arrest. What I needed was to know where in the world was the rest of the stolen car.

That evidence did not come and I was at a dead-end. So the time came to apply the pressure to Eddie. He was on probation for a previous criminal act, so after speaking with his probation officer, the officer told me to pick up Eddie and we would interview him.

I knew I had enough to charge Eddie with the stolen hood, but I wanted the rest of the car, and if I didn't handle this just right, I would more than likely lose it.

Eddie was brought in and told he was going to be charged with possessing a stolen hood and that his probation was going to be revoked and back to jail he was going.

Things would be a lot easier if he told me the whole story. At first I could tell he thought I was bluffing and had nothing on him, but as time went on, I could see the wheels turning in his head and he was calculating how to get his best deal.

Eddie was rather flabbergasted that I was basing my whole investigation on an extra hole in the hood of his restored Firebird. But he finally gave it up after negotiating with the probation officer.

It turned out that Eddie did go to the victim's house a couple of times, and he learned the victim's pattern of when he would be and not be home. Eddie stole the car and drove it to his house. In one night, he stripped it and took all the parts he needed.

What he did with the rest of the vehicle makes any person who loves muscle cars cry.

Any part that would burn was put in a pile and burned. The frame was cut up in small pieces and placed in a junkyard in Detroit, along with any other unused metal parts.

After getting the confession and dealing with Eddie, I called the owner of the stolen vehicle.

When I told him what had happened to his prize Firebird, he did all he could to fight back the tears. He could not believe someone would actually cut up a car, use the parts, and throw away the rest of it. But that is what happened.

After the conviction in court, restitution was ordered and Eddie had to reimburse the owner of the Firebird. I thought it would be poetic justice if Eddie had to turn his Firebird over to the victim. But that didn't happen.

Just another day in Waldo County.

The Camaro

Back in 1996, Chevrolet decided to stop producing the full-size Chevrolet Caprice police package. The Caprice had been the choice of cruisers for the Maine State Police for a good 15 years by then, and Chevrolet's decision to stop making the full-size police package caught our department off guard.

The lieutenant in charge of the state police fleet decided to try different avenues and was willing to experiment with some extraordinary vehicles.

One decision was to purchase police package Camaros. Eight of these vehicles were bought, and one was assigned to each troop in the state. This spread the cars throughout Maine and allowed everyone to see them.

The Camaro was a very sleek sports car. Camaros were powered with LT-1 Corvette engines and were extremely fast and powerful cruisers. There were four colors purchased—blue, white, red and black. It was a real attention-getter, even more so than a regularly marked-up state police cruiser. These Camaros had blue lights on the roof, decals on the front, rear and sides, and included a special decal about the DARE program.

To put it simply, it was visually very sharp and impressive. And the car drew attention no matter where it was. A stop for gas usually meant an extra 15 minutes for curious people to look at it.

After they were purchased, the department looked to assign the Camaros to one trooper from each troop. When I heard about this, I jumped at the chance to be considered. I wrote a memo explaining all the reasons why I thought I should have the cruiser.

As luck would have it, I won out and got the Camaro that was assigned to Troop D. I was absolutely elated to have this for a cruiser. So much so that when it became available to be picked up, it was in the middle of December and there was a major snowstorm blowing through Maine on that particular evening—but I wanted that car.

I had this vehicle for the next year and a half and, as a result, I have many stories involving this cruiser. I thought I would share one with you.

One particular evening, I received a call from Maine State Police headquarters to respond to a domestic dispute at a China residence. The female had left the home and gone next door to her father's house to call the police and to stay safe until the police arrived.

The caller said she had been assaulted, and that her boyfriend, "Chuckie," was extremely intoxicated and argumentative.

I was vaguely aware of who the parties were. Before my arrival, the male called in and reported that his girlfriend's father had come onto his property and blown a hole through the front door of his house with a 12-gauge shotgun.

The father, who was listening to a scanner, then called and said his daughter's boyfriend, Chuckie was the one who had shot his own front door, and was trying to blame him.

I had also spoken with the female complainant before my arrival and learned Chuckie had been arrested in the last month for another domestic. I learned too that when the officers had dealt with that incident, Chuckie had taken a swing at one of the troopers, and run into the woods, where he was later apprehended. So, it looked like I was going to be dealing with a fighter at the very least.

I finally arrived at the residence. It was actually quite easy to find, as it was the house with a huge hole in the front door that you could throw a basketball through. I pulled into the driveway, got out and entered the house from a side door. I carried my six-cell flashlight with me. Chuckie met me at the door, and I asked him what had happened that evening.

Chuckie was very drunk, which was a good thing for me as I noticed that Chuckie was rather muscular and looked like he might go rather dry [put up a fight]. He was right on spin dry and started complaining about his girlfriend and what she had done to him.

I then explained to him what his girlfriend had already told me, which wasn't good. Chuckie then sat on the living room couch, and I could tell he was calculating what to do next.

About this time, I advised Chuckie that I was going to be arresting him and taking him to jail in Augusta. He jumped off the couch, bounded over to me, got right in my face and screamed, "Oh yeah, you and what &@*$^/# army is taking me to jail?"

I took a rather defensive position, cocking the six-cell flashlight with my right arm behind my back, ready to strike if he so much as took any type of swing at me. Then I told him it would just be me and my Camaro lugging him to jail.

He looked at me in total disbelief and asked, "What did you say?"

I told him again that me and my Camaro would be taking him to jail.

He asked, "A Camaro?"

"Yep, a Camaro."

Chuckie ran to the door, saw a nice shiny red Camaro sitting in his driveway and asked me, "You're taking me to jail in that car?"

"Yep, I am," I said.

"Well, let's go," he responded.

So I handcuffed Chuckie, took him out to the Camaro, and loaded him into the front seat of my cruiser, and off we went to the county jail.

We ended up talking about the Camaro all the way to Augusta and he told me that he never had a better ride to jail than that one.

Just one of the many stories with my Camaro.

Pig Pile

I thought I would share a story that includes my good friend, Warden John Ford, and another guy who never seemed to figure out when to keep his mouth shut. His name is Walter.

Walter is a special person if there ever was one. He was brilliant when it came to intelligence, but he lacked common sense. He would rather do things the wrong way and try to get away with it, than apply his knowledge the right way.

I knew if he did things the right way, he would have been extremely successful. However his big downfall was alcohol. And when he drank, he thought he was invincible, able to outsmart any cop.

One nice summer morning when there wasn't much going on, I was on patrol and wrapping up loose ends of cases. I was near Brooks and knew it was Warden Ford's day off and that he would be at home.

John was starting a calendar business adventure that would include his beautiful wildlife drawings. John told me that he needed quiet time at his kitchen table to look out over the hills of Brooks and finish the sketches. I knew he was so looking forward to his day off to do this new endeavor.

I thought it would be fun to go to his house, get some hot chocolate and see how he was making out with his drawings. Just before I made it to the downtown intersection, I saw a group of men at a residence. They were hanging around a vehicle with its hood up.

I immediately recognized the men—Walter was one of them. Over the years, I had lugged most of them off to jail. They too, recognized me.

Good ol' Walter turned toward me. With his left hand he held up a can of Budweiser and with his right hand he gave me the finger. You just don't know how hard it was not to give it right back at him. But being the professional and taking the high road, I simply smiled, albeit a little smugly, and waved a friendly wave.

I continued to John's house and pulled into his dooryard. His garage door was open, so I backed my cruiser around and parked half in-half out of his garage. I was still stewing that Walter had given me the finger and that I could not do anything about it.

John had all his drawings on the kitchen table and he was looking out over the hills. I admired his art work and sat across from him so I could not see the road. I placed my portable radio on the kitchen table so I could listen to State Police headquarters in case they needed me.

I started to explain to him about the incident downtown. John chuckled and told me not to get him worked up; he said this was his day off and he needed a calm, steady hand to draw. I, of course, continued on with the story just to needle him.

"Well speak of the devil, here he comes," John said.

"You're kidding," I said and turned to look at the driveway. Sure enough, there was Walter and his girlfriend driving a car into John's dooryard.

From my observation downtown, I knew Walter was drunk and his visit at the Ford compound was not going to be a pleasant one.

"Wonder what he wants," John asked as he got up from his chair to meet Walter at the door.

Walter had made his way inside the garage, standing at the kitchen screen door. In his drunken stupor Walter demanded, "I want to know why that cruiser is backed into your garage."

"None of your business, Walter," John replied.

I had gotten up from the kitchen chair and was listening behind the wooden kitchen door.

"I am a taxpayer of this state and I demand to know why that cruiser is parked inside your garage," said Walter.

John's reply was something that I should not write. But I can tell you the conversation was going nowhere fast. From behind the door, I whispered to John to tell Walter that he had to leave the property.

John finally figured out what I was telling him to do. So John, in only the way he can, said to Walter, "You take both your hands, put them behind you, grab your butt cheeks as hard as you can and get off my property."

This infuriated Walter. I again told John to tell Walter to leave his property and if he refused, that he would be arrested.

"You can't arrest me. I'm a taxpayer and I have a right to be here," Walter sputtered.

"Tell him one more time, John," I said.

John gave him one more warning and Walter flatly refused to leave. "I ain't going nowhere," he said, defiantly standing in the same spot.

He had his warnings. John opened the door and we both went through it on the fly. Walter was at the bottom of a pig pile so fast that I still don't think to this day he knew what struck him.

I quickly handcuffed Walter and arrested him for trespassing on John's property. I loaded Walter into the front seat of my cruiser and started the trek to the county lockup in Belfast. His girlfriend sat in her car shaking her head in disbelief.

It would be fair to say Walter was not very happy—he was spitting, sputtering and cussing at me. He called me names that even I had never heard before. And he was screaming it in the front seat of my cruiser. After several miles of listening to him, I thought I would call dispatch at State Police Augusta and tell them I was taking a prisoner to jail in Belfast.

Walter, though, would not be quiet, so I called on the radio while he was bellowing. The words and names that came over the radio for those few moments will be remembered for quite some time in radioland.

After a long silence from dispatch, dispatcher Bill Grosser finally inquired "434, are you all set?"

"10-4 Augusta, I'm all set," I replied.

Walter was booked and placed in the drunk tank until he sobered up, which probably took a few days. I did my paperwork and when leaving the jail, I realized I had left my portable radio on John's kitchen table. So I drove back to get it.

I tried to quietly retrieve my radio from his kitchen table but John was still wound up like a top.

"You know, Nickerson, this was my day off. I was at home, minding my own business, having a nice, quiet day doing my drawings and you came to town and stirred up the pot! I just got calmed back down after you left and was starting to draw again when your radio went off and that idiot was calling you names over the radio. I got wound up all over again. I will never get these drawings done."

"Oops, sorry," I apologized as I grabbed my radio and ran laughing out of his house.

Just another quiet day in Waldo County.

Those Damn Motorcycles

Some of the most gut-wrenching, edge-of-the-seat escapades troopers get into are high-speed chases.

While extremely controversial, a high-speed chase is a tool that should never be taken away from law enforcement. It seems as though every time I was involved in chases, most of the comments were positive and supportive. But there was usually at least one person who criticized the practice of chasing the bad guys.

The Maine State Police always had a chase policy and you had to follow the guidelines set forth in it. The most important was that if the danger of the chase outweighed the safety of the public, then we had to call it off.

This was the officer's judgment call. The supervisor also closely monitored chases, and if he believed the chase was too dangerous, he could also call it off.

I cannot count how many times I was involved in pursuits, but I remember every one of them in vivid detail.

Many ended peacefully when the offender realized he was not going to get away. But a good many also ended in crashes. Seeing a crash right in front of your eyes is certainly an attention-getter. How some people ever walked away without being hurt was amazing.

Believe it or not, some chases were quite humorous. I thought I would share one that at least ended rather comically, although it wasn't funny when it was happening.

I had worked the day shift on a hot summer day. It had been so busy that I never made it back to the summer cottage until almost 11 p.m.

When I arrived, all I could think about was getting something to eat. As I looked through the cupboards, I knew I was either going to bed hungry or I had to go into Augusta before the last restaurant closed.

I knew Friendly's on Western Avenue was open until midnight, so off I went with a friend to see if I could get there before closing time.

I didn't bother to change out of my uniform, and I jumped into the cruiser and headed in. The ride into Augusta was uneventful as I made my way up Western Avenue, turned into the far left lane and stopped at the stoplight in front of Friendly's.

It was a beautiful warm summer night and there was still a lot of activity on "the strip." It seemed like a long time waiting for the green arrow to light up, and my belly was growling.

A set of traffic lights was just behind me, and I could tell the lights turned green and traffic was coming my way. I heard the scream of a motorcycle behind me. It was one of those "crotch rockets" and it was coming very fast. I thought to myself, "Is this guy going to see the cruiser and at least slow down when he goes by me?"

Apparently not. That missile shot by me at least 70 mph while I sat at the intersection. We were in a 25-mph zone, and I knew without a doubt that I was not going to get anything to eat that night.

I quickly took off after the rogue motorcycle and chased it up Western Avenue. The thing I hate about bikes is that they can weave in and out of traffic and accelerate so quickly that it can be difficult to stay with them.

I didn't bother putting on my blue lights initially because I wanted to see if I could at least get close enough to stop the driver.

The bike got caught in a bit of traffic and I got in behind it and turned on my blue lights. At that point, if there were no other problems, it was a speeding ticket.

The passenger on the bike noticed the blue lights flashing, and I could see him tap the driver on the shoulder and point in my direction. The driver turned and looked right at me. This is good, I thought. He has seen me and is going to pull over and stop.

That was not what he had in mind, though. He simply turned back around, lowered his body and took off at an even higher rate of speed, weaving hrough the cars that had slowed him in the first place.

Vehicles in front of me pulled over and I was able to take off after the bike, keeping it in sight. I saw it take a side street to the right and go up Blaine Avenue. I turned and at least stayed with the biker as he made his way up the side street, ran a stop sign and continued.

I also could see the passenger wanted no part of the crazy ride. He beat on the driver, trying to get him to stop—but to no avail. I knew the area well and knew we were coming to a T-intersection by Camp Keyes in Augusta. Beyond the T-intersection was a tall cedar hedge with a cemetery beyond the hedge.

The bike was going way too fast to be able to make any type of turn at the intersection. The poor passenger was still beating on the driver as it approached the intersection.

After that, it was all dust. I saw two guys and one motorcycle flipping occasionally through the air when they soared higher than the dust cloud.

I stopped in the intersection and looked around. The bike had crashed into the very tall cedar hedge and the driver was getting up to run.

I ran after the driver, grabbing him and bringing him back to my cruiser. I was still in disbelief over the whole thing as I put the suspect against the hood of my car to search and secure him before checking on the passenger who, by the way, I still could not see.

Just as I had finished handcuffing the driver and the dust had settled a little more, I heard a guy yell. "Geeoorrggeee! What are you trying to do, kill me?"

Out from under the cedar hedge, the passenger came crawling on his belly like he was crawling through the jungle in Vietnam. He was pulling himself along by his arms, and he wasn't all too happy with the driver. He inched closer and cussed up a storm at the reckless driver.

I had already called for an ambulance and Augusta police. They arrived just in time as the passenger made it to my cruiser.

It turned out, after being examined by the ambulance personnel, he was just too drunk to walk.

It was a different story for the driver. He had just been released from prison. The motorcycle was stolen, his license was suspended, he was operating under the influence of alcohol, and he was on probation with many conditions. Strike five, he was out.

He went straight back to prison to serve the remaining seven years of his sentence. He was lucky he didn't kill anyone during his brief furlough.

I never did get anything to eat that night. Probably a good thing.

Just another quiet evening.

Special Assignments

I recently went through my father's police belongings and notebooks. I should tell you that my dad became a Maine State Trooper in 1953, was one of the original Maine State Police detectives in February 1955 and he retired as captain of the Criminal Division in 1973.

One of my dad's mentors was a trooper by the name of J. Edward "Eddie" Marks. Eddie was one of the original Maine State Police troopers when the department was formed in 1925.

Eddie served the citizens of Maine for 50 years, retiring in 1975 as commissioner of Public Safety. Eddie Marks was, to say the least, about as colorful a character as there ever was.

In the early days of the Maine State Police, motorcycles were used to patrol, and Eddie carried around his 350-pound pet bear, "Minnie" in the sidecar.

Can you imagine!?

As I was going through some of Dad's scrapbooks, I came across a story written in 1985 by Karen Lemke, author and daughter of Eddie Marks.

She has written two books about murder cases during her father's career. They are great reading and include information about our state and the history of the department.

One of the many duties of Maine State Police officers is being assigned to executive protection when dignitaries, including United States presidents, visit.

Maine detectives work closely with the Secret Service to take care of concerns during the dignitary's stay. While I was reading this story, I became amused by it and thought it would be nice to share.

It goes to show how things have changed over the years.

I am enclosing the following story about my father, Ret. Capt. Millard E. Nickerson, and Ret. Commissioner J. Edward Marks (both of whom have passed on).

I should also tell you that when Eddie retired in 1975, he was considered one of the deans of the state police nationwide. Quite an accomplishment.

State Police veteran recalls special assignments
By Karen Lemke
Reprinted with permission of the author

Maine hosted a string of newsmakers over the years, from performers to presidents. State Police security for visiting dignitaries made its debut in 1927 when Charles Lindbergh was escorted from Old Orchard Beach to Portland following his solo Atlantic flight. Franklin Delano Roosevelt's 1941 arrival in Rockland from the Atlantic Charter Conference was still another step in solidifying the Secret Service role of the Maine State Police.

By the time Richard Nixon arrived in Maine in 1952, the Maine State Police were used to the security function. One of the most familiar was Captain J. Edward Marks, who had orchestrated virtually every major security detail since Lindbergh's.

Doubling as security and driver, Marks met Nixon in Rockland. Due in Augusta at an appointed time, Nixon was behind schedule when he boarded the waiting police cruiser.

By nature a laconic sort, Nixon rarely made small talk. But on this occasion, his speechlessness was involuntary. With Marks behind the wheel and Nixon lodged in the back seat, the cruiser flew up Route 1, scattering everything in sight to safer ground.

By the time the police car shot over Route 32 to Augusta, Nixon was riveted to the seat gripping the armrests, uttering only a "yes" or "no" to Eddie's occasional inquiries. Now, Route 32 is known for its curves, dips and hairpin turns, and Nixon was fast becoming acquainted with each one of them. Immobilized with fright, the Vice President could not have been happier to see the little capital of Augusta, Maine, and on time.

Some years later, in 1960, Nixon again visited the state, and who should he meet but Capt. Marks. Eddie extended his hand and prefaced the greeting by, "You don't remember me, do you?"

Turning to his aide, Nixon gasped, "My God, not him again!"

A smile flickered across Nixon's face as he clasped the driver's hand who'd given him the ride of his life, probably only paralleled by a spin with Leonid Brezhnev, who careened Nixon around Camp David years later.

During a 1964 visit to Maine, Lyndon B. Johnson attracted the largest crowd Portland had ever seen, and that proved to be another security test. Nearly 100,000 enthusiastic spectators made the President feel at home, even though he was in an overwhelmingly Republican state.

Perhaps it was his rugged but pleasant demeanor which appealed to Mainers. Perhaps it was a feeling of friendship and support that symbolized Maine's aversion to the Dallas tragedy.

Finding himself president and a contender as well, Lyndon B. Johnson was gearing up for the approaching 1964 election. It was 10 months after Dallas when Johnson came to Maine. He was the first incumbent president to campaign here since William Howard Taft visited Portland in 1912.

State Police Capt. J. Edward Marks was undercover for Johnson and could have been a distant stand-in for him. Fond of Stetsons decades before the Western mania swept northward, Eddie sported Lyndon B. Johnson's cranial trademark—and with all the familiarity of the latter. It did not go unnoticed by the President, who commented to Marks, "I didn't know there were two of us."

Johnson reached City Hall Plaza for his campaign speech. If the crowd was exuberant, the same adjective applied to Lyndon B. Johnson, who lent a personal touch to his presidential visit. Even before he started speaking, Johnson spotted a sign being waved in front of him proclaiming: "Lisbon Falls Needs LBJ."

The Androscoggin County town of Lisbon Falls was in tough straits with its mills shutting down and businesses folding. Calling for the sign, the President had it handed up to him on the platform and waved it as the crowd roared back its approval. Calculated to whip up his audience, he added, "No one would dare offer handouts to the people of Maine."

The audience was in a festive mood and gave the President a wild, loud and heartfelt ovation. Many times during his 30-minute address, President Johnson was halted by bursts of applause. Now he had a dose of northern hospitality.

But while he was spell-binding his audience, the White House team was figuring how to bind him. The mob scene could result in a nightmare, and LBJ's chanting was working the crowd into a frenzy.

One of the Secret Service advance men approached State Police Detectives Millard Nickerson and Eddie Marks. "We need a favor from you boys. Things are getting out of control and he's got to be rolled to that elevator. But he'd know what we were doing and we could be fired on the spot. We don't dare do it, but he can't touch you."

Nickerson and Marks exchanged knowing glances. Chaos would result if Johnson got out to the stands, and the same would happen if his advance prevented his cakewalking.

"Sure," Nick replied, and he and Marks shook hands with the advance teams as they positioned themselves.

Sure enough, just as he finished his speech, Johnson stepped forward, but that was as far as he got. Like moths to a light, the Maine State Police encircled Johnson and rolled the protesting President to the city hall elevator.

"Didn't he holler and screech," recalls Nick. "If he could have fired us, we'd have been finished on the spot. We did our part and got him to the elevator. The doors opened and there inside was the White House team. They didn't have to touch him. We just spun him into their arms as he was giving a final blast of, 'Let my people come'."

Misplaced Trust and a Timely Tip

This story sounds like it came right out of the Wild West.

And it demonstrates the dangers that police officers can face each and every day doing their job.

What some people will do to avoid capture is unbelievable and sometimes civilians and officers are severely injured or killed. Thankfully, no one was seriously hurt or killed in this episode, but a cruiser and a stolen vehicle were destroyed.

It started innocently enough when two people from Hancock County crossed paths. One was an elderly well-to-do gentleman who had a nice home and possessions on the coast.

The other was a spoiled young charmer who wanted to get rich quick. The younger man saw the older gentleman as an easy target for robbery. Late one night, the young man put his plan into action. He went to the older gentleman's residence on the ocean, tied up the man and his wife, rummaged through the home and stole whatever he wanted and whatever else he thought would bring a good price.

Lastly, he took the gentleman's Mercedes-Benz. It was a nice little coupe that was fast and maneuverable—certainly capable of outperforming our cruisers.

Leaving the couple tied up, the young man headed along the peninsula to a route that would get him out of the area. There was one problem: he didn't tie them up quite well enough and the couple freed themselves fairly quickly. Police responded to the residence and after a preliminary investigation, put out a bulletin over the police radio for law enforcement to be on the lookout for the stolen Mercedes.

Bucksport Police spotted the vehicle and tried to stop the driver. But the young man had other ideas, outran the cruiser and headed into Waldo County.

The suspect was flying south on Route 1 and each police from several departments along the way commenced to try to pull over the motorist, with no success. The driver of the Mercedes ran through roadblocks and avoided apprehension.

Not only had the young man committed felonies at the original site of the robbery, but each time he ran a roadblock, he was committing another felony. It was getting more serious as he kept fleeing.

In Belfast, the young man again ran a roadblock. Belfast had more than one cruiser and the chase continued along Route 3 toward Augusta. The Belfast officers could not overtake the fast Mercedes, but they could keep it in sight.

A call was placed to Maine State Police headquarters in Augusta. Trooper Tom Ballard's residence was west of the chase. Tom was asleep when the phone rang, alerting him to the chase that was coming right at him.

Trooper Ballard jumped up, threw on his uniform, and took off in his cruiser. He made it to the end of his road, as it intersects with Route 3, just in time to see the blue lights of the approaching Belfast cruisers.

Tom pulled out and got up his speed to stay in front of the suspect vehicle. As his speed increased to well over the speed limit, Tom did his best to keep the Mercedes behind him, but to no avail.

The Mercedes driver pulled alongside the cruiser and the young man rammed the side of Ballard's car, trying to force him off the road.

Trooper Ballard was fighting to stay on the road when he was struck again. This time, the bumpers locked together and both vehicles, with the Mercedes in the lead, left the road, went into a ditch and hit small trees, causing both vehicles to roll.

The Mercedes rolled on its roof and Ballard's cruiser rolled on its side. Trooper Ballard thought this would be his time to grab the guy. He tried to unlatch his seat belt, but couldn't.

He was so twisted and hung up with his weight against the seat belt that it would not release. All Trooper Ballard could do was watch as the suspect jumped out of the Mercedes and took off on foot.

Belfast police officers helped Trooper Ballard get out of his cruiser, but they didn't catch the bad guy that night.

The next morning, I came back on duty from a day off. Before signing on, I received a call from Maine State Police headquarters in Augusta of a burglary in the Belmont area.

I had no idea of the happenings from the night before, but a dispatcher filled me in about the chase and where it had ended. This burglary could well be connected to the robbery suspect.

I went to the residence of the reported burglary and met with the homeowner. He had heard about what had happened in the neighborhood the previous night and thought that this burglary might be related.

The homeowner had an outbuilding used primarily for storage with a bed and some clothes. There were wet clothes on the floor that had obviously been put there recently. The homeowner knew what clothes were missing from the building, and this gave us a new description of the suspect and what he would be wearing.

The clothes left behind matched the description of the clothes worn by the suspect involved in the high-speed chase.

I was parked in the driveway of the residence of the burglary just feet from Route 3 and was clearly visible to traffic passing by. I was outside the cruiser talking with the victim when a passerby stopped. He interrupted my conversation to give me some information.

"Are you one of the troopers looking for a robbery suspect?" he asked.

"I am, but how in the world would you know about us looking for a robbery suspect?" I asked.

"Well, I live in scanner land and have been listening to the police radio traffic all morning. I just want you to know that I was at the 10-4 Diner in Montville and a young man who was very nervous approached me wanting a ride. I refused him, but when I got back in my car and heard all the traffic, I thought this might be your guy. Actually, I am quite positive it is the guy you're looking for."

"What's he wearing?" I asked.

The passerby described a man wearing the clothes missing from the burglary scene. The passerby said he had left the 10-4 Diner within the previous 10 minutes.

I was quite sure the young man at the 10-4 Diner was our guy. I put out the information over the radio and fortunately Trooper Louis Nyitray was in the right place at the right time.

Nyitray later told me he could not have gotten the information at a more opportune time. He was minutes from the restaurant on Route 3 and as he approached, a man fitting the description of the suspect was coming out the door of the diner.

Nyitray pulled into the parking lot and stopped within 50 feet or so of the suspect. With his gun drawn, Nyitray ordered the suspect to get down.

Long story short, it was the person for whom we were looking. With assistance from the Waldo County Sheriff's Office, the suspect was taken into custody and transported to Waldo County Jail.

There is a moral to this story, sad as it is. Unfortunately, it is a mistake to become friendly too quickly with people we don't know. The elderly gentleman thought he was helping a younger man, but all that really happened was the elderly gentleman became an irresistible target for the suspect. Please be careful out there.

Just another day in the life.

"Flick My Bic"

One of our favorite fishing holes to look for OUIs in Waldo County was the 10-4 Diner on Route 3 in Montville. This establishment was clearly a favorite place for many people to go to and have a grand old time.

There was plenty of music, sometimes by famous musicians such as Boxcar Willie, lots of dancing, some fighting and, of course, a whole lot of drinking.

One of the many problems facing law enforcement officers when the place let out was there were never enough troopers to patrol the area.

Within a very short distance from the hall, traffic could go in five different directions. But we dealt with it the best we could and after learning the habits of many of the patrons, we got smarter dealing with the traffic flow.

One particular early morning, I had made several stops, had checked several operators' sobriety and had removed one drunk driver from the road. The traffic stops had taken me several miles from the establishment.

When I finally cleared the last OUI stop, I worked my way back to the club, only to find it completely empty and shut up tight. That was the routine each night anyway— traffic trickled out initially, then bam, everyone left the dance hall at once.

I drove into a store parking lot from the west and looked over the area to see if there was any more traffic.

While checking this all out, I noticed a flicker of light in the middle of Route 3 to the east, almost at the top of the hill.

I thought to myself, "What in the world is that?"

So I pulled out of the parking lot and drove toward the light.

As I got closer to the flicker of light, I began to make out what it was. It was a little old lady, well into her 70s, sitting in the middle of the road.

As I pulled up beside her, I noticed she was dressed in a white jumpsuit, her hair was neat, and in her right hand she was holding a lit Bic lighter, which she was waving back and forth.

I also noticed a stream of liquid underneath her, streaming along the middle of Route 3. At first I thought she had put a bottle of beer in her pants, but seeing no bottle, it could only mean one thing. Yup, she was relieving herself on the yellow line in the middle of the road.

I could tell without speaking with her, that this was one very drunk lady.

I thought to myself, "This is going to be fun."

My first concern was to get her out of the road before some unsuspecting person hit and killed her. I flipped on the cruiser's blue lights to warn traffic. I then rolled down my window to speak with her, expecting a very funny lady, especially after seeing her in this predicament.

I nonchalantly asked, "What'cha doin'?"

She replied with slurred words, "I'm trying to find my way home!"

"Are you having any luck," I asked.

My expectations then took a nosedive. What I got back was a stream of expletives that would embarrass the most hardened of people.

She let loose a barrage of swear words and told me just where I ought to go and on and on and on. Well, this wasn't what I had expected. And I didn't really want to go where she was telling me to go, either.

So I asked her name, to which she replied, "None of your $%&*# business."

So it was going to be one of those. Back then, we did not have the public drunkenness law, so I could not take her to the lock-up.

The only avenue I had was to find out who she was and get her home. However, I did not know who she was and she was not making it easy for me.

So I loaded her into my cruiser (after I covered my seat) and went back to the club to see if I could find someone, anyone, who knew her.

I was out of luck. There was absolutely no one around, and no lights were on at any of the nearby residences. I kept asking myself, "What am I going to do with her?"

It was getting to be 3 a.m. and I was stuck with a belligerent, soaked drunk in my cruiser. I finally had enough and as much as I hated to, I called a contact in Liberty who knew everyone in the area. I went to his house and he came out to the cruiser. After one quick look at her, he started laughing.

My friend told me I had "Mrs. Smith" and then he told me where she lived with her kids. I couldn't thank him enough and off I went to deliver the "package."

I pulled into her yard at about 3:30 a.m. and some lights were on. "Mrs. Smith" was too drunk to navigate her way, so I left her in the cruiser and went to get her family (which I was quite happy to do, due to what she was putting me through).

I had her son come out to the cruiser, first to make sure that I had who I thought I had, then to have him help her into the house.

When we got back to the car, I asked him if she was his mom and he said she was. I then proceeded to tell him what the last 90 minutes had been like with her and that he needed to get her out of my cruiser and into the house.

He looked at me with the saddest eyes and asked, "Do I have to?"

To which I replied, "Yes!"

Seems no one wanted old "Mrs. Smith."

Quite frankly, I understood why.

Just another quiet evening.

The Tree Blew Up

As I have mentioned before, removing drunk drivers from our highways was perhaps the biggest goal that I had throughout my career. I was always on the hunt for drunk drivers when working, no matter what else I was doing.

I also learned that drunk drivers provided a lot of entertainment. There are lots of stories to tell and this is one of them.

One Friday, early in the evening, I got a call to respond to an accident on Frye Mountain in Montville. This is an area where there are a lot of nature enthusiasts, hunters and hikers. To be called to an accident on the mountain is somewhat unusual, so when I was en route, I thought that something unusual could be happening.

I arrived at the crash site and met with the operator of the pickup truck. His name was "Bert." Right off, I could tell Bert was very excited, quite intoxicated and happy to see me. He was happy to see me as he was scared to death.

After telling me his story I could see why. His vehicle was well off the road and smashed into a tree down over an embankment.

When investigating such incidents, I usually would ask what happened and let the operator tell the whole story from the beginning to end before going back over it. This gave me a base to work from while trying to figure out the details.

After making sure Bert was not injured and not in need of any immediate assistance, I had him get in my cruiser so I could speak with him.

I started with the usual, "So what happened?"

Bert started to explain that he was out drinking after work and went up to Frye Mountain where it was a safe place to ride around and drink. Not much traffic, as he said.

Bert was to meet some other friends up on the mountain later, so he thought he would get there before them. While traveling up the mountain he came upon a tree across the road that he could not drive around. So Bert stopped his pickup and got out to remove the tree from the roadway.

Bert approached the tree, bent over to grab it and started pulling it out of the way. All of a sudden, KABOOM!! Bert told me that the tree blew up. It scared the living crap right out of Bert. He screamed, ran back to his pickup, turned around and took off at a high rate of speed to get the hell out of there as fast as he could.

While traveling way too fast down the narrow road to escape, Bert lost control of his pickup, went off the road, down over the embankment and crashed into a tree.

After Bert told me his story, I just sat there kind of taking it all in. Now, I knew he was intoxicated, and that he definitely had too much to be driving, but after his story I began to think that he was way more drunk than I originally thought.

So I started to ask Bert questions to get more specifics. I asked Bert if that was exactly what happened and Bert replied, "Yup."

"Well, Bert, let's go back to that part about the tree blowing up. You said the tree blew up as you were trying to remove it from the roadway?"

"Yup."

"Well, Bert, what do you mean, 'the tree blew up'?"

"The tree blew up!"

"Could you be a little more specific?"

"It just blew up!"

"Well, how did it blow up?"

"It just blew up!"

I explained to Bert that trees just don't blow up, and I wondered if Bert had taken a few of those mind-altering, hallucinating-type drugs.

Bert told me that he did not do drugs, and that the tree blew up.

I then told him I was taking notes and this would be brought up in court sometime in the future. Bert assured me that he was telling me the truth. So I had Bert tell me again what happened. True to form, he told it just like the first time. Again, I had to go back to the tree-blowing-up part.

"OK Bert, just explain the tree thing one more time."

"I got out of my truck, I approached the tree to remove it and when I grabbed it to pull it out of the way it EXPLODED!!"

"OK Bert, if this is your story, then this is your story," I said. "I'm not too sure I would tell many people about it, though."

I asked Bert for directions back to where the tree "blew up" and he gave them to me. After processing Bert for the drunk-driving charge, getting his vehicle towed and getting Bert to a safe place, I went back to Frye Mountain to further investigate. Somehow I had a difficult time believing what Bert had told me.

I located the area where the tree incident reportedly occurred. A crew of National Guardsmen was at the site. Then I thought, "What the heck?"

I got out of my cruiser and could see a tree blown apart. There were some ranking officers with the National Guard and they were also looking over the scene.

I asked them what they were doing there and the major told me that his unit was doing a drill on the mountain over the weekend.

I explained to him that I was there investigating a motor-vehicle crash involving a tree that had blown up. After I told him this I could see the blood drain out of his face.

The major told me that an advance team had come up on the mountain ahead of the regular unit and had set a number of booby traps. It was to keep the regular unit on high alert so it would be ready for anything.

So I asked about the tree and the major told me that it was a booby trap and it had been tripped.

About all I could do then was shake my head and chuckle. Poor Bert had told me the truth. I can only imagine what he was thinking when this tree actually did blow up.

Just another quiet evening.

The Christmas Present

This might be hard to believe, but some people take advantage of just about anything to get away with something they have done wrong.

Back in the early 1980s, I even ran across someone who took advantage of Christmas. The only thing I give this criminal credit for is he never intentionally hurt anyone. But he was notorious for committing property crimes from which he could monetarily benefit. I'll call him Eugene for the purposes of this story.

Eugene was a unique person. He was intelligent and he let people know right away that he was. He hated authority and bucked the system every chance he got. But the thing that always brought him down was he loved to drink. I can hardly remember any time I had contact with him when he wasn't inebriated.

Except on this particular day.

The incident started earlier in the year when the old Stink Factory in Brooks was broken into and a business checkbook was stolen. At first, it was a real whodunit and I worked the case as time allowed. We figured it would only be a matter of time before some of the checks started being cashed.

Right we were.

Usually when this type of crime takes place, the checks are made out for small amounts of money. Not this guy, however. He went for the big bucks, cashing checks for hundreds and thousands of dollars in large stores. He even used or borrowed someone else's identification and driver's license. After following the leads, it became obvious the main suspect was none other than my old buddy, Eugene.

So I approached him and started to put the squeeze on him. Of course, I got the reaction I was expecting—total denial and bewilderment. But I knew it was him, and I made sure he knew it.

What I needed was the checkbook to seal the case. By letting Eugene know he was the prime suspect, I knew he would quickly make a move with it.

Having worked the case so diligently, I had earned the trust of some of Eugene's friends. They did not like what he was doing and they wanted to help me.

Early one morning, I got a phone call stating Eugene was taking the checkbook to another town to hide it. The tipster stated it was wrapped as a Christmas present in the car Eugene was driving from Unity toward Windsor at that very moment. I jumped out of bed and took off to find Eugene. I located him just north of Albion and made a traffic stop.

Eugene was alone in the vehicle, and we exchanged our usual pleasant greetings, which were really not very pleasant at all. I then told Eugene why I had stopped him.

He acted all aghast and vehemently denied the checkbook was in the car, or that he had anything to do with the stolen checkbook at all.

Walking up to the car I had noticed a wrapped Christmas present on the back seat. It was shaped just like the checkbook I was looking for. I told Eugene that I was going to search his vehicle for the checkbook, and he arrogantly stated, "Go ahead, you won't find it here."

So I started looking through other things knowing full well it was the present. While I was looking, I mentioned to Eugene the present in the back seat sure looked like it could be a checkbook.

I could tell this bothered Eugene, who said he would never disrespect Christmas and that it was a present for his niece. I told him I needed to make sure it was only a gift and not a checkbook. This put Eugene on spin dry. Inside, I really hoped Eugene would not stoop low enough to use Christmas to cover up a crime.

We reached for the present at the same time and both had a hold of it. We were two grown men standing beside a vehicle on a main road, each of us grabbing an end of a Christmas present.

Eugene hollered at me to let go of his niece's present.

I, on the other hand, did not let go, and it turned into a tug of war. About that time, I let my finger slip into the side of the wrapping paper and tore it open. All I could say was, "Eugene, you bought a checkbook for your niece? How nice of you!"

Eugene was speechless.

"Thanks for the present," I told him, "and seeing how it is so close to Christmas, you are not getting arrested for the burglary and theft and forgery today, but after Christmas, expect a visit from me. This is my present to you, today."

For once, old Eugene didn't have anything to say. He just got in his vehicle and drove away.

Merry Christmas, Eugene! Just another day in the life of a trooper.

We Do Chase

Perhaps some of the most hair-raising experiences on patrol occur during high-speed chases. Over my career, I was involved in many, many chases with varied outcomes.

The training we received at the Academy was excellent—it covered departmental policy, a week on the driving range learning to operate cruisers at high speeds, and training on how and why to end chases. The most important decision is left up to the officer and supervisor, and that is: Do I chase or not chase?

While on routine patrol at night, I often checked a local store at the head of China Lake. I always worried about the store being robbed at night. I also knew a lot of drinkers got their alcohol there when the other establishments were closed for the evening. So it was also a good place to look for drunk drivers.

On this particular evening, I approached the store from a side road and noticed a motorcycle leaving the store from another entrance.

There were two people on the motorcycle and they turned to travel away from me. As the motorcycle turned onto the highway, the operator had a difficult time balancing the bike, and it almost tipped over. This made me wonder if the operator had been drinking and I thought I should check further to make sure he was safe.

I knew the operator had not seen me yet, so I continued past the store to get behind the motorcycle. I again noticed the operator was having a difficult time keeping the motorcycle in a straight line. As I pulled up behind the bike to activate the blue lights, the operator looked behind him and noticed me. With this, he leaned forward, downshifted and off to the races he went.

The bike was an older motorcycle, a Honda 750cc, and it went pretty good but nothing like the rockets of today. We went through some turns and his speed picked up to 70, then 80 and then 90 mph.

After the turns, the road straightened out for a long stretch and I pulled up alongside the motorcycle. He seemed to be topped out at a speed of 91 mph. I kept looking over at him and tried to make him understand that he was not going to get away from me and to just pull over, but he seemed to have different ideas about the situation.

We traveled side by side for some distance, with the cruiser's blue lights and siren activated. Way up ahead I noticed a vehicle going in the same direction as we were, traveling in the motorcycle's lane. I thought this would force the biker to slow down and stop, as I had him blocked from coming into my lane, and the car ahead would keep him blocked in as well.

Boy, was I in for a surprise. Before reaching the vehicle, the motorcyclist, at 91 mph, moved into the breakdown lane and was readying himself to pass the vehicle on the right.

All I could think of was that we were going to scare the hell out of the people riding in that car. However, there were still more surprises ahead.

Just before I caught up to the vehicle, its driver saw my blue lights and pulled into the breakdown lane to let me go by. Well, you can imagine what happened next. Yep, the motorcycle ran smack into the back of that vehicle at 91 mph.

What I saw next you only see in the movies. Both the motorcycle and passengers went airborne over the vehicle and flew through the air for what seemed like several hundred feet. I was stunned watching this through my side window as I traveled along beside them. The motorcycle came down first, landing in the ditch, and the two occupants came to earth another 50 feet beyond the bike, bouncing and sliding along the ground before coming to rest.

I was certain these two people were dead. Before coming to a stop, I called for an ambulance. I screeched to a halt and ran to check on them.

Then I got another surprise. Neither of them was seriously hurt! They were obviously shaken up and had some road rash, but they were not hurt badly. Of course, the motorcycle did not fare so well; it was totaled.

You have to understand that a police officer's stress level gets pretty high in situations like this, and to say the least I was pretty excited. Well, so was the operator of the motorcycle and his passenger, who turned out to be his girlfriend.

After making sure everybody was OK and that help was on the way, the operator screamed at me, "Why the hell were you chasing me?"

"Why wouldn't you stop for me?" I threw right back at him.

To which he replied, "I'm from Portland, and they don't chase. All we do is downshift and accelerate and they won't chase."

"You're not in Portland," I told him. "You're in the country, and we do chase!"

After investigating the matter thoroughly, it turned out the guy had been drinking, his license was suspended and the motorcycle was stolen. Which just goes to show, you never know what is going to happen when on patrol.

A Grassy Thanksgiving

It was the middle of a Thanksgiving night in the early 1990s. I had no immediate family to spend time with, so I tried to take most of the calls in the Waldo County area so other troopers could stay in with their families and enjoy the holiday.

It was well after midnight and it was very quiet; there was absolutely no traffic on the road. My area covered all the corners of Waldo County, as well as a couple of towns in Kennebec County. It was a large area and I traveled a great deal to respond to calls. A lot of the time, or should I say just about all the time, high speeds were involved when responding to the calls.

On this particular Thanksgiving night, I had to travel across Route 3 from the Belfast area to China. It was not an emergency, but due to the long distance, no traffic and the good road, I had picked up my speed.

Traveling across Route 3, I made note of several things as I skipped along. One rather eerie thing was I had not seen a vehicle since leaving Belfast. I had just gone by the state park on Lake St. George in Liberty and was on a long straight-away when all of a sudden headlights appeared way behind me. Not only did they appear, but they were gaining on me. I knew this vehicle had to be traveling in excess of 100 mph.

At the speed I was traveling, no headlights should be appearing behind me, let alone gaining on me. I decided to watch for a minute or so, but the vehicle was coming toward me faster than I cared for.

Rather than do a reverse clock, I wanted to lock this vehicle onto my radar. And the only way to do that was to get way ahead of the suspect vehicle, get into a position off the road, turn around and get the radar pointed at the suspect vehicle. I raced for the boat ramp on Sheepscot Lake, a spot I knew would work well. I got there in time so the suspect vehicle could not see my cruiser's tail lights turning off the road. I shut down everything awaiting my prey. I didn't have long to wait.

The suspect vehicle screamed right at me. I wanted it to get close enough so when I turned on the radar, it would have a good signal and I could instantly lock in the speed, just in case he had a radar detector. The moment came, I turned on the radar beam and bam—105 mph.

I quickly turned on all my lights, along with the blue lights, and started after the suspect. I thought it was going to be a long pursuit, but the vehicle immediately pulled over and stopped. And I pulled in right behind it.

It was a black Monte Carlo with Massachusetts plates. You never know who you are going to make contact with, so I looked things over pretty good before approaching. It could have been as simple as a family returning home to Massachusetts. They could have been in a hurry and thought they could make up time while traveling the back roads of Maine before getting on the Interstate. I made note, however, the operator was alone in the vehicle.

I approached the driver and he rolled down his window. I could have fallen over from the cloud of smoke that hit me. Wafting out of the vehicle was enough smoke to make me think he was burning a field inside of his car— a whole field. And it wasn't a hay field he was burning either! I looked at his eyes and there was no doubt this guy was higher than a kite. I could not help but ask him what in the world was he doing.

"Oh, just heading home to Massachusetts," he replied.

"Are you in a hurry?" I asked him.

"Yeah, kind of," he said.

"So you're heading to Massachusetts, smoking dope and driving 105 mph. You don't think you might draw some attention to yourself, do you?" I asked him.

"Never really thought about it," he said.

I had him get out of his vehicle, as he was going to go to jail for the speed and for operating under the influence of marijuana. With the door open and the operator stepped back from the vehicle, I noticed a half-open black duffel bag in the back seat.

"What's in the bag?" I asked my suspect.

The guy went pale and started shaking all over. Without me even looking in the bag he said, "Take the bag and everything else, just please let me go."

"So what's in the bag?" I asked again.

This time, no reply.

So I reached in and brought the bag outside. Inside were two solid bricks of marijuana, along with a whole bundle of cash. I looked again at my suspect and asked what it was. I thought this guy was going to pass out. He was shaking, all the color in his face was gone and his voice was cracking.

Again, he told me to take the bag and the money and there would be no questions asked; it would be like we never saw each other.

I looked at him with great big eyes and asked, "Are you trying to bribe me, too? Don't you think you're in enough trouble already?"

"You're going to arrest me, aren't you?"

"Of course I am," I informed him.

So I handcuffed my suspect, finished searching the vehicle and after having it towed, carted my suspect to the county lockup in Belfast. We had quite the conversation on the way to jail, but the only thing he would tell me was that he came here from Massachusetts, made a purchase in Belfast and was on his way back to Massachusetts when I stopped him.

He also told me that he knew I was only a road trooper and if he was going to make any deals he wanted to talk with a drug enforcement officer. I told him he might regret that later but that was fine and I would set up a meeting while he was in jail.

It's funny how you can build rapport with someone in a short amount of time. I treated him decently, but he knew he was in a world of trouble. I did my job and put him behind bars, and I treated him with dignity.

The next day, I made the arrangements with our drug people to go to Waldo County Jail and interview my suspect.

He, of course, was looking for the best possible way to deal with the trouble he was in, which meant he was going to have to spill the beans about his contacts.

Arrangements were made and I sat in on the interview. The drug agent came on strong, not believing anything the suspect had to say. They got into a hollering match, with the suspect getting very angry. He knew he was not getting anywhere with the agent. The agent was clearly playing the bad guy to get under the suspect's skin, but to me it looked like it was backfiring.

I thought for sure the suspect was going to shut down and tell us nothing. After about a half-hour, the agent got up and walked out. The suspect hung his head, not knowing what to do. I could tell he did not like the agent and he didn't want to give his information to him.

So I told him, "I'll give you one chance to tell me everything, or I'm walking and you can deal with the agent."

"You'll do that for me?"

"Yes, I will, but you have to give me everything. And it better check out."

By the time the agent returned to the interview room, the suspect had told me who the contacts were in Belfast, and the other towns in Massachusetts. He was only a courier but kept good information on the people he was dealing with. The agent was surprised, to say the least, that I was able to get that information from the suspect so easily.

For me, it's all in how you treat the people.

This case turned into a fairly large multi-agency drug investigation that brought down a lot of dealers. And best of all, the money confiscated was turned over to the state, which was used to purchase more equipment.

Just another quiet Thanksgiving evening.

Treated Like a King

Being the old man with lots of seniority in Troop D certainly had its benefits. It usually put me at the top of the list to be called for details available to troopers. I could pick and choose what I wanted and what fit into my schedule quite nicely. And there were a lot of details available.

I liked doing a variety of things rather than the same details over and over. Escorting pre-fab homes from Jackman to anywhere in the state became one of my favorite things to do as I got to see parts of Maine that I didn't see very often. Ship launchings at Bath Iron Works were also great because of the diversity at one event. I could see the marvels of modern technology, the people who supported them and the protestors who did not.

Another favorite was presidential details. When George Bush No. 41 was president he, of course, had his summer home in Kennebunkport. The Maine State Police helped with security whenever President Bush stayed at his compound. We worked closely with the Secret Service, and even though we never got that close to the president it was an honor to be able to do such a duty. We were working on the spot where history was being made.

In addition to details for President Bush No. 41, I also did details with Presidents Reagan, Clinton and Bush No. 43.

In the summer of 2000, I had an opportunity to do a detail that involved former President Bush and his wife, Barbara. I jumped at the chance. It involved a couple of motorcades, a luncheon, a speech and seeing them off at an airport. I shined my shoes extra well for the detail, in case we came close to the Bushes.

The beautiful summer day arrived and I went to Camden to hook up with Lt. Jeff Trafton and then we went to oceanfront homes. We connected with the Secret Service agents who traveled with the Bushes.

The cottage and the scenery on the ocean were breathtaking. The agents laid out the details of the day and what our duties were. I tried not to think of all the bad things that could happen, but they were in the back of my mind. I tried to enjoy the detail for what it was—I was about to spend the day with a former president of the United States. What an honor.

The first thing we did was get things in order, and we got ready to take off at a moment's notice. We knew the Bushes were having breakfast and taking in the ocean view. After breakfast, the Bushes were given a tour of the main house and grounds.

The complex was absolutely stunning. It had beautiful homes and cottages, immaculate landscaping and breathtaking views. Plus, the garages housed an extensive automobile collection—something that I was looking forward to seeing, if possible.

We escorted the Bushes to the main house near the top of the property. We took up a strategic location between the main house and the garages. While I was waiting, a gentleman came out of a garage and said he worked on the automobiles. It was a pleasure meeting him; he and I had a lot in common. I love special-interest American automobiles, and this man had a wealth of knowledge and worked on one of the finest car collections in the country.

The gentleman heard I was going to be involved in the detail and, knowing my love of cars, offered to give me a walk-through of the garages. He took me into one end — the Buick garage. There, lined up one after another, were Buicks from each year. Each one was better than new.

In the Chrysler room I noticed that no matter what year the vehicle was, it had a matching year license plate. Even the license plates were restored to new condition. I couldn't help but ask the man about the plates. I got bold and told him I had a 1956 T-Bird and asked if he had any extra plates for that year, kind of chuckling about my request.

Of course, I was only joking and not expecting anything, and he just smiled. The former president was also getting a tour of the vehicles, and so I abandoned my tour. I went back to my post with Lt. Trafton while the Bushes toured the garages.

What happened next will stay with me for the rest of my life. This president was down-to-earth, cordial and very friendly. While standing beside my cruiser with Lt. Trafton, the Bushes walked up one of the driveways. As they approached, President Bush asked his wife, Barbara to get out her camera and take a picture of him with the troopers.

I immediately got a little nervous. It wasn't every day something like that happened. President Bush came over to us, shook our hands, and thanked us for protecting him and his family. He stood between Lt. Trafton and me while Barbara Bush snapped several pictures of us. Then the president asked Barbara to give the camera to someone else and have her picture taken with us also. So she did.

After all the photos were taken, I expected the president and his wife to continue the tour. Not so. They stayed and engaged us in small talk. Finally, President Bush asked me for a business card.

I had to ask, "Why do you want that?"

The president responded simply, "How do you think I'm going to get the photos to you?"

Of course, I was expecting an aide to do all the behind-the-scenes work. Nope. The Bushes did it. The president had me write our names and home addresses on the

business card and he took the card with him. All I could think to myself was: "What a truly kind and down-to-earth couple."

After they left, the man from the garage presented me with a restored 1956 Maine license plate. He told me it was a gift. I was all smiles and quite dumbfounded. That gift is still on my 1956 T-Bird, one of my prized possessions.

Soon after, we took part in a motorcade to Point Lookout in Northport. Our job was to get the Bushes into the complex, where they were to give a speech to MBNA employees. Once they were inside and all was secure, the Secret Service said it was time to take a break and have lunch. Set up on the enclosed deck was a lunch prepared solely for us. I dined on lobster rolls, fresh salad, desserts fit for a king and choice of many beverages. This was like being in another world. I could not believe how extravagant everything was.

After we finished lunch and the Bushes had finished their speeches, we participated in a motorcade to the top of the mountain to a private office with a 270-degree view of the ocean.

We were high on the mountain, and the office had a private conference room, a large entranceway and all glass facing the ocean. Some displays included model ships in huge cases—things I had never seen before. Alongside the building was a helicopter pad with a waiting helicopter. We brought the Bushes to the building for a tour, then to the helicopter for departure. It was amazing to see the Bushes get into the machine and see it lift off, put its gear up and fly off the mountain toward the ocean to take them to their plane. I was in utter amazement about the whole day.

I reminisced all the way home, thinking of the wonderful day and of meeting a former president of the United States. Sometimes it was just hard to call what I did work.

As a footnote to this story, I did receive the photos from the Bushes. They both autographed the photos, which are some of my favorite photos from my career.

Learning From Old-Timers

As I have shared in previous stories, removing drunk drivers from our highways was one of my highest priorities throughout my career with the Maine State Police.

Removing them from the roads was both rewarding and, in a lot of instances, entertaining. This particular drunk driver fell, literally, into both categories.

Late one weekend night in the 1980s, I was traveling across Route 3 in Searsmont. We called this particular place the devil's triangle, because so many bad things happened in this small area.

As I was driving west, a vehicle went by me in the opposite direction. Something about the way it was being operated caught my eye. As soon as I got out of sight, I flipped around and pursued the vehicle to pull it over.

The operator must have noticed he had met a cruiser because he took off to get out of the area as quickly as possible. I always like to think the police have an edge on drunk drivers right from the beginning—they are drunk, and we are sober.

The speeds picked up to over 100 mph quickly, and the chase was on. We were eastbound and I was gaining quickly on my prey. One problem with chasing someone is that you have to react to everything the suspect throws at you—and you never know what they might do.

This particular chase did not last long as I was able to quickly close in on the suspect. He probably thought he could not shake me. But all of a sudden, the suspect screamed the vehicle into a long driveway, slammed on the brakes, and skidded to a stop at the edge of the lawn adjacent to the woods. Before the vehicle even came to rest, the driver's door flew open and out he jumped. He went on a dead sprint into the woods. He was running a lot faster than I thought I could run.

"Oh great," I thought to myself. If there is one thing I hate to do, it is run, but after the short car chase my adrenalin was pumping and I jumped out of my cruiser as well. Armed with my flashlight, off I went to apprehend the bad guy.

Or so I thought.

As I said, running was, and is, not one of my strong points. And I was in such a hurry that I had not called the car chase or the foot chase in to Maine State Police dispatch. I was on my own. As I ran into the woods, I thought I would just stay with him and wear him down and he would give himself up.

So I ran along behind him about 20 feet or so and was doing pretty well. I had the flashlight right on him and I kept pace with him. I may have even gained some on him.

We had been running for a while and I was feeling a little winded, or maybe even a lot winded. I started to think that I had to end the chase quickly or I would lose him.

So as I kept the flashlight on him and ran along behind him, I remembered a story an old-timer told me about chasing a night hunter through the woods in pitch darkness.

The old-timer realized he was lighting the way for the bad guy to see while he was running away from the law. So the old-timer shut off his flashlight and the next thing he heard was a loud thud. When he turned the flashlight back on, the bad guy was knocked out cold from running into a tree. The old-timer was Warden John Ford. It was hard to believe most of John's stories, but this particular one came to mind and I thought I would see if it could work for me.

So I turned off my flashlight. And it was textbook. The next thing I heard was a loud thud, a very loud groan, and another thud. I turned my flashlight back on to see my bad guy flat on his back, half unconscious and bleeding from his forehead. Apparently the second thud was him hitting the ground backwards.

His noggin had just smacked into a very large pine tree, and he was feeling the effects of it. While he was half-conscious, I thought it was a good time to handcuff him, then catch my breath.

It seemed to work out fine. He came to after I had caught my breath. I helped him up and escorted him back to my cruiser so we could take a ride to the county lockup. And patch up his head.

The Hungry, and Cross, Drunk

It was June 1979 and I sat in my cruiser one evening in a service station parking lot at the base of Moosehead Lake in Greenville.

A friend had stopped and we chatted as I watched traffic go through town. As my friend drove off toward the Junction, another vehicle pulled into the parking lot and stopped right behind my cruiser. The driver tooted the horn at me, or so I thought. I was familiar with the driver, Bernie, and had some minor dealings with him, but I couldn't imagine why he was honking the horn at me.

So I got out of my cruiser and approached the driver's door of his vehicle. Bernie was plastered and I told him I needed to see his driver's license and registration.

Bernie reached into the glove compartment, grabbed a handful of papers, put them in front of his face to look at them, then threw them all around the inside of the car. I thought to myself that this was not going to be good.

A little about Bernie. He was not from the area and had a sordid life before he arrived in Greenville. As far as I could tell, he was pretty much continuing the same type of lifestyle in Greenville.

I also knew he worked out. Once while responding to his residence, I noticed his weights outside. They consisted of a solid steel bar with five-gallon pails of cement at each end. Even the bar was bent from so much weight. So I knew he was quite strong, and he sure looked it—he was built like a barrel.

So here I was with him in a parking lot. He was very drunk and I knew things were going to get worse. After he threw the papers throughout the car, he looked at me and said, "I can't find them."

"Well why don't you just get out of the car then, Bernie," I told him.

Bernie jumped out of the car and stood between the door and me. Once he gained his balance he started to flex his muscles. Then he said, "I dare you to arrest me. I could kill you in one swipe!"

"Yeah, you probably could, Bernie, but you are under arrest for drunk driving," I replied.

"Wait, wait, wait. Can't we talk about this first?" he asked.

I think I took him by surprise by telling him so quickly that he was under arrest. So I said we could talk about it and told him to get into my cruiser where we could do just that.

We both got into the front seat, with me behind the wheel. As soon as I sat down Bernie's face was glued to my chest.

He was growling like a grizzly bear in heat and chewing. I could not imagine what he was doing, so I backhanded his head to get him away from my chest and we both got out of the cruiser and met at the trunk.

Bernie was wound up like a top and we went toe-to-toe. I grabbed him by his muscle T-shirt and when I grabbed it,

Bernie pulled away and I was left holding the T-shirt in my hand. Bernie then took off running across the road.

I took off after him and caught up with him on the other side of the road. Well, as we got there, Bernie tripped, fell and landed on his stomach. I thought I was going to be able to restrain him, but I fell too and landed right on top of him.

Bernie screamed, "I give up!"

But I rolled right over him, which allowed him to get up and run the other way, right back at my cruiser.

Seeing as how this was happening in the middle of the town of Greenville, a small crowd had gathered, including a local Greenville officer.

I will never forget that poor, short man trying to block Bernie in the middle of the road. When Bernie barreled into him, he knocked the officer on his rump, and his revolver went flying.

However, the collision did slow Bernie down just enough for me to catch up to him again. As we made it to the front of my cruiser, I tripped Bernie. And when he fell his head went right through the front grill of my cruiser.

Bernie was more than stunned, which gave me an opportunity to start handcuffing him, which I did. However, he started to stir before I could get the second one secured and the struggle was on.

That's when Bud, the Greenville officer, came over and we were finally able to get the other cuff on. Bernie was so bulked up that it was almost impossible to do so. We then placed Bernie in the back seat of my cruiser and I heaved a sigh of relief. I felt like I just wrestled a 500-pound bear.

Cpl. Paul Davis arrived and he asked me in his dry way, "Young fella, what are trying to do now?"

"Well, Paul, why don't you look in the back seat and you can see what I've been doing!"

Bernie looked like an irate caged animal. He pumped up his muscles, snorted like he was trying to break the handcuffs and screamed at me to uncuff him so he could get a drink of water.

I calmly told Bernie that I didn't think the cuffs were going to come off. Even Paul looked at me and said, "Don't take the cuffs off, we'll never get them back on."

Paul locked up his cruiser and told me he'd better ride to jail with us. It was almost a 40-mile ride to jail in Dover and, trust me, I welcomed the company while I transported Bernie to jail.

Bernie quickly passed out and I described the melee to Paul. I also told him Bernie had gnawed at my chest, but that I hadn't felt anything. Well, after getting to jail, I finally knew why.

After placing Bernie in the drunk tank, I pulled my Cross pen out of my front shirt pocket to fill out some paperwork. It was then I noticed the pen was almost chewed in half. Cross pens are made out of plated steel, and Bernie's teeth marks were clearly visible. Then I knew what Bernie had been trying to do to me, but he got my pen set instead. Thank heaven for that pen set. If Bernie had got a hold of my chest, he would have bitten a chunk right out of me.

A footnote to this story: After Bernie was convicted in Superior Court, he was ordered to pay restitution for my pen set. I did keep the original as a souvenir.

Just another routine OUI.